Soul-Made
Recognising and Upholding Human Creations in the Age of AI
by Vanya Rani Leonard

First published in German in 2026

ISBN: 978-93-5592-255-7

International Edition, 1st edition, June 2026

VANYA RANI LEONARD

Soul-Made

Recognising and Upholding Human Creations in the Age of AI

Soul-Made

Who are you when you use AI

– and who will you become as a result?

Who or what will we become,

when we outsource creativity?

CONTENTS

PART 3: TRUTHS AND OPPORTUNITIES

PART 4: RE-ORIENTATION AND OUTLOOK

PREFACE

AI has long been part of our everyday lives, making it increasingly difficult to tell what is still human-made. For the first time in history, we have digital tools that appear to think and create for us. Perhaps now is the right moment to remember the extraordinary capacities that come with being human.

The question is no longer how quickly technology is advancing, but rather this: how much of our lives are we willing to hand over to AI – especially our creative expression? What do we gain? And what do we lose? More importantly, who do we become? Will humanity dissolve into simulation, speed and sameness, or will we remember our deeper needs and strengthen our soul-informed abilities? What choices will we make as creators and consumers?

Creativity, once the most unique and meaningful feature of human life, is now not only challenged but also imitated. Images, songs, films, books and poetry – works once born out of enthusiasm, passion, longing, pain or inner necessity

– can now be produced in milliseconds. Flawlessly. And endlessly. Chatbots, image generators and other AI systems are mimicking tasks we have always associated with human intelligence and inspiration.

Some call this progress. Others feel unease. I find myself asking: How do we preserve what is naturally alive in us instead of outsourcing it to generative AI like ChatGPT, Claude, Gemini, Grok or Midjourney? And how do we know what lies behind a creation today, whether it is human, AI-generated or a hybrid – and whether the resonance surrounding certain content comes from people at all?

I use AI myself at times. Its output can be helpful, but also incomplete or simply wrong. Generative AI can check spelling, correct grammar, translate text, suggest structure, detect patterns and provide summaries. Yet over time, I became aware of the danger of being seduced by seemingly perfect results. I began to notice how easy it was to lose touch with my own way of knowing and my own voice. More about my journey with generative AI in Chapter 12, *Own Voice over AI Polish*.

I realised that the deeper question is not about the tool itself, but about us. About our attitude, our self-respect and our willingness to stay awake in a world that increasingly encourages us to go on autopilot, delegate our responsibilities or allow others to tell us how to live and what we should consider meaningful. What happens when we start to delegate our perception, judgement or creative capacity to some authority outside ourselves? Who must we become in order to meet AI well? As our tools become more powerful, human maturity becomes more, not less, important.

The book offers practical guidance. I point to the subtle ways AI has already entered art, design, business, consulting, therapy and spirituality – fields that overlap and shape our attention, identity, values and decisions. I examine where AI is used behind the scenes and sold as human work, where education risks becoming dangerously superficial and where our health, trust and sense of reality may be compromised.

Above all, I want to help you protect your creative spirit and sharpen your discernment, so you can make informed choices as a creator and as a consumer. Whatever you choose – organic or synthetic – choose consciously.

I wrote *Soul-Made* to spark a conversation about how we can recognise the human signature in a time when nearly every aspect of life is being digitised and delegated. To affirm that authenticity is neither a luxury nor something negotiable, but essential for our culture and our consciousness. To show how important creative self-expression is for our well-being.

This is a call to honour human creations that are infused with lived experience and original insight. To honour the gift of being human. Let us not casually surrender the gifts we have been given. Especially since we have only just begun to explore and cultivate all dimensions of our human potential.

The journey within, not the journey outwards, is the gateway to our greatest possibilities.

We do not need perfection. We need what is real. And we need it now.

Vanya Rani

INTRODUCTION

Once upon a time, not so long ago, people made things. With their hands. With their hearts. With their minds. With their spirit.

Originality was easy to recognise. It carried human fingerprints. The paint smudge at the edge of a canvas. Deliberately unfinished brushstrokes. The unusual phrase in a manuscript. A cheeky twist, an unexpected element of chaos or humour in a plot. The nervous cough during a live presentation. These irregularities were not flaws. They were proof of authenticity. And that is precisely what made our work beautiful, real and relatable.

Fast forward.

Today, with a few clicks or voice commands, you can generate a perfectly photorealistic sunset that no one has ever seen, create a new version of yourself using selfie apps and filters, produce a flawless love ballad on a gadget that has never loved and publish an entire book without ever having thought a complete sentence yourself.

It is a remarkable achievement. And it is not without risk.

Because while synthetic generation becomes sleeker by the second, the human touch is slipping away – that slow, natural and deeply personal process of creation.

In a world where AI can produce stories, symphonies and strategies, what happens to artists, composers and designers who love their craft passionately, who have studied it for years and matured into mastery?

And something else has shifted. AI is no longer simply a tool that responds. It is beginning to act.

AI agents – synthetic actors that can post, reply, comment and connect with one another – move through digital spaces and shape opinions and culture. When realities can be manufactured this way, the question becomes more urgent: What is being amplified? What is disappearing? And what suddenly comes to be seen as normal?

These are important questions because culture shapes reality. And reality, in turn, shapes us. The more we live alongside simulations, the more our perception adapts to the synthetic.

The global trend points towards an ever-deeper entanglement of human beings and technology. We are witnessing new dependencies, new professions and new ways of living that are influenced and co-created by pre-trained AI systems and digital infrastructures.

What risks arise when someone seeking healing ends up with a "certified practitioner" who was trained exclusively through AI-generated online courses without disclosing that background? What happens when we stop asking where something comes from, who made it, how it was made, with what attitude and level of understanding? What happens to those who outsource their creativity and become trapped in algorithmic labyrinths?

My concern is clear. Some readers may not agree with all of the conclusions I draw. And at times, this book may feel confronting. This is not meant as an attack or a judgement, but as an invitation to look more closely at how we create, choose and consume. An invitation to reflect: What exactly are we doing? And why?

Soul-Made is not intended to fuel endless debate, but to encourage discernment, solution-oriented dialogue and freedom of choice.

This book is a call to preserve human creativity and its process when more and more people focus on instant rewards and AI polish. It is about remembering what it means to be soulful and to create something that is truly soul-made.

One way to better understand where we may be heading is to look at what happened to food. Several decades ago, industrial food processing promised us convenience, abundance and efficiency. And it delivered. But at a cost. Processed food became normal and what was once simple and alive became technologically engineered, standardised and addictive. Only later did a counter-movement emerge. Organic food, slow food, local produce. We witnessed a return to what is real.

So, this book seeks to offer: ways of recognising the difference between highly processed and organic forms of expression. A language for describing synthetic perfection and navigating this new reality. Tools for strengthening trust in your own senses and perception. Clarity about what you wish to delegate to AI and what you do not. Above all, it invites us to rediscover and cultivate the capacities that make us uniquely human.

AI can simplify workflows and reduce tedious tasks. But there is a line we must not allow it to cross, otherwise we risk losing ourselves. That is when creative people become mere operators of systems and their true selves begin to fade. At the very least, we should have a fair chance to compete when we create naturally. And we should be able to make informed choices when we consume.

Just as farmers once fought for the right to label genuine food as organic, we now face the bizarre reality of having to defend the validity of human-made work. A time when books, paintings and music may require "organic" labels confirming that they were made by people rather than bots and programmes. Or perhaps one step further: When human beings themselves might require a "non-GMO" or "Heirloom" badge to confirm that they have not been genetically modified.

Let that sink in for a moment: we have reached a point where we need to certify what is simply natural. That alone reveals a fundamental shift.

And although this book sounds the alarm, it also seeks to illuminate a path forward. A path where technology supports human creativity but never replaces it. A path where we choose human-made or human-led work where it matters. Where we celebrate soul-made art in the same way we celebrate *farm-to-table* food or *bean-to-bar* chocolate because we recognise its excellence, appreciate its richness and defend its value.

I defend what makes us human. Our wonderful irregularities. Our inner and outer beauty. Our imperfect expressions. And our endearing moments of stumbling, followed by acceleration when understanding suddenly clicks.

Life is a process. A continuous unfolding and becoming. We do not honour life by avoiding this process. We honour it by participating in it fully. It is not about consumption, control, speed and perfection. It is about awareness, mental agility, inspiration, contribution, exchange, devotion and working in harmony with nature.

And the crucial question is this: **Who are you when you use AI – and who do you become as a result?**

Which naturally leads to another question: **Who or what do we become when we outsource creativity?**

Creativity is, at its core, pure life force. And like all life force, it seeks expression. The same energy that creates life also longs to express itself through thoughts, words and actions. This is where human-made creation comes from. And I wonder what happens to human potential when the capacities through which it matures are gradually delegated elsewhere.

It is one thing to be creative with AI. It is something entirely different to create from within yourself and be transformed in the process through the eureka moments, the struggle, the discarded attempts, the inner listening, the discoveries and the gradual maturation.

Welcome to Soul-Made – Recognising and Upholding Human Creations in the Age of AI

WHAT IS AT STAKE

One side effect of generative AI is the growing doubt surrounding every published work.

When I read a good piece of writing these days, there is often a quiet suspicion that it may have been written by AI. I love books and I love reading, but this doubt changes something. At times, it spoils the entire experience and the relationship I have with an article, essay or email. It can almost be compared to the feeling of suspecting deception without being able to prove it.

Yet my unease does not end there. There is another layer to it, one that is almost never mentioned in the glossy AI narrative. When I learned that generative AI models are built with the help of content moderators and data labellers who filter vast amounts of toxic material, I was left with a sense of discomfort and a dilemma. More on this in Chapter 16, *Who Feeds AI and Supplies the Ingredients*.

AI tools absorb and recombine existing information and create an encyclopaedic pool of data that can be immensely useful.

Yet they can also inherit distortions or produce homogenised outputs that shape our perspectives and decisions. Over time, this influences our culture and our reality.

The more we use these digital systems, the more our frame of reference shifts, often without us noticing. Our perception changes, our expectations change. And with them, our work.

I keep noticing this shift in everyday situations. I experienced it again not long ago. It is a telling example of how we currently handle our data, images and privacy.

It happened at my photographer's studio. I asked his assistant for passport photos, which he took with a digital Canon. Instead of loading the image files into a photo editing programme, he dragged the selected image directly into ChatGPT. It happened so quickly that I barely realised what he was doing. I immediately said, "Stop. Take me out of this GPT chat. Now." He looked confused. I repeated, "Take me out of this GPT window. You do not have permission to upload my image into any AI application." He searched the menu, unsure. I raised my voice. The photographer stepped in, took over the computer, deleted the chat and began editing the image in the classic, professional way.

What does this episode show?

That AI is already being used reflexively, even where it is neither necessary nor appropriate. That the work itself is no longer considered. AI has become a default tool for tasks that were previously handled with specialised, non-generative software.

And that our images can, within seconds, end up in systems without our consent, over which we have no control. Neither over how they are processed nor where they go next. Data protection seems almost a thing of the past. Not out of ill intent, but out of convenience, habit, dependence or naivety and lack of awareness.

Against this backdrop, another movement suddenly gains significance: a turn towards the natural. In this era of digital saturation, soul-made could be the last rebellion left to us.

Perhaps it looks something like this:

- Music that preserves the vibration and tone of a real human voice.
- Art that still carries the scent of paint-stained hands. Studio and atelier visits.
- Stories infused with wisdom, humour and lived experience.
- People coming together to exchange ideas and brainstorm. Different insights. Many perspectives.
- Craft and professional tools, digital as well as analogue, consciously chosen. Skill, experience and care.
- Products and solutions developed by people who see the bigger picture and also take the details seriously.
- Healing facilitated by people who have walked their own healing path. Not linear. Real.
- Guidance offered by people who genuinely meet you rather than merely respond to you.
- Like-minded people, neighbours, friends, family. Conversations. Laughter. Cooking. Playing. Sitting together.
- Nature. Seasons. Harvests. Things you can touch, smell and taste.

Every tool, whether a sword or a technology, has the capacity to serve or to destroy. It depends on who wields it.

And so another question is this: How do we remain conscious of the power we hold?

Are we guided by love, truthfulness, moderation, composure, integrity and humility? Or by convenience, greed, the pursuit of power, perfectionism, ego and the illusion of control? Whatever our motivation may be, it has consequences.

To me, soul-made means a creation that arises from lived experience and fresh ideas.

Natural creativity is not a nice-to-have. It is psychologically necessary, both for us as individuals and for us as a society.

In the traditional philosophy of India, this creative power is described as *Shakti* (the Sanskrit word for primordial energy and creative force). It brings ideas, fertility and potential into manifest form.

When we outsource creativity to AI, we are not just outsourcing work. We are outsourcing our development. What is at stake is our humanity and our becoming.

"Nothing in the human psyche is more destructive than unrealised and unconscious creative impulses." – Marie-Louise von Franz, classical philologist, psychoanalyst and collaborator of C. G. Jung, *Spiegelungen der Seele* (1978)

Either we create consciously or the unconscious creates through us. Because creativity does not disappear when it is suppressed, left unexpressed or outsourced. It simply changes form. And it can become destructive.

There is another distinction between AI-generated output

and genuine creative development. If highly processed culture becomes the norm, human-made expression may become a speciality: rarer, slower, more expensive and more precious.

And so this book is my contribution to what is alive, creative and beautiful. To what nourishes, connects and brings order.

It is written for the creators, the thinkers, the visionaries, the feelers, the persistent ones and for all those who refuse to let the real, raw, wonderful and sometimes painful aspects of being human be sterilised or erased.

For those who understand that great art is not born through speed and polish, but through a creative process and the unique energetic signature of the artist.

PART 1

THE ORGANIC ANALOGY

CHAPTER 1

THE ORGANIC REVOLUTION THEN
A MODEL FOR CREATIVES TODAY

In the beginning, everything was organic. Food grew from the earth under open skies and was tended by calloused hands. The harvest may not have looked perfect – crooked carrots, uneven tomatoes, sun-scarred apples – but it was alive. It had aroma. It nourished. It healed.

Then came the industrial food revolution.

Crops were bred for maximum yield, grown in greenhouses, sprayed with chemicals and engineered into perfect uniformity. Food became plentiful, predictable and pretty. But it also became less nutritious, less flavourful and less real. I remember a moment in a London supermarket almost twenty years ago when I saw a plastic tray of tomatoes with a sticker that read: "grown for taste". The very fact that taste had to be emphasised felt disturbing.

I still have the sobering book *Eat and Die* by Udo Pollmer and Eva Kapfelsperger, first published in 1982 in Germany. Meticulously researched, it describes conventional and alternative agriculture as well as health risks hidden in our food: heavy metals, psychiatric drugs and other toxins.

The turning point came when consumers began looking for alternatives to fruit and vegetables that barely smelled or tasted of anything. Vegetables that seemed to last unnaturally long and tasted frustratingly bland, as if coming from a laboratory.

So began the organic revolution. A movement of people who wanted their food the way nature intended it, healthy and full of flavour.

Consumers demanded:
No pesticides on vegetables.
No chemical coatings on fruit.
No hormones in milk.
No synthetic additives in bread.
No genetic engineering in seeds.
No chemical colourings in sweets.
No flavour enhancers in spices.

What began as a niche movement became a global one. Organic farmers, once dismissed as idealists, became pioneers of food integrity. Labels such as Organic, Non-GMO and Farm-to-Table became trusted marks of quality and symbols of authenticity and naturalness. Organisations such as Demeter, Ecocert and Bio Suisse became internationally recognised standards for genuinely organic, wholesome products.

Today, a remarkably similar dynamic is emerging in the creative realm. Just as consumers rejected chemically altered food, people are beginning to notice the blandness and confusion that can arise from synthetic forms of expression.

Artists, musicians, photographers, writers and lifestyle influencers, as well as service providers in business and career consulting, fitness, healing work, coaching and therapy, are increasingly using AI, often without disclosing this to their clients.

And just as, a few decades ago, we turned to farmers' markets and slow food to reclaim the integrity of our meals, we may now need a movement for organic creativity. One in which real, heartfelt, soul-informed and human-crafted works are valued, encouraged and protected.

The lesson from the food industry is clear: we began labelling what was natural when the synthetic became the norm.

And perhaps today we must do the same for books, music, photography, paintings and professional services – with signs of authenticity that attest to their human origin.

CHAPTER 2

AN ASSORTMENT OF APPS
BOOM IN SYNTHETIC EXPRESSION

In the early days of artificial intelligence, creative expression seemed like the last bastion of humanity. After all, could a technology ever write a novel that makes us weep? Paint a landscape that makes us dream? Or create music that touches our deepest longing? Many believed it was impossible. Then it did.

Suddenly, AI could generate entire books and training courses, create realistic watercolour paintings and compose songs within seconds. It could imitate styles, copy famous artists and even write in the voice of authors long deceased.

And consumers loved it. It was fast. It was affordable. It was flawless. It was astonishing. It carried the appeal of novelty.

Yet just like highly processed food, highly processed content comes at a cost. One arrives looking perfect but offering little nourishment. The other arrives perfectly formed and may reach the mind, but does not necessarily nourish the soul.

AI novels follow flawless narrative arcs, yet they lack lived experience. AI-generated images may look breathtaking, yet they lack the unique energetic signature of a real artist. AI-generated therapy may imitate compassion, but it can distract us from our inner knowing. AI-generated followers and reviews deceive, distort reality and create unfair competition.

We risk living in a world where media content becomes as homogeneous, glaring and antiseptic as the fast-food chains lining our motorways. A world in which artistic diversity and uniqueness are filtered out and replaced by algorithmically polished uniformity.

This development is not only visible in what we consume, but also in how we think, learn and express ourselves. Even fundamental human abilities are beginning to shift.

A widely shared report refers to a survey conducted by the University of Stavanger, suggesting that a significant proportion of Zoomers (Generation Z, born between 1997 and 2012) struggle with handwriting. In many schools, cursive writing has already been abandoned, as though it were little more than a nostalgic ornament.

But there is more to it. Handwriting activates the brain. It slows thinking down just enough to deepen understanding and strengthen memory. Experiments by Pam A. Mueller of Princeton University and Daniel M. Oppenheimer of Carnegie Mellon University show that handwritten notes support complex understanding and conceptual thinking more effectively than typing on a keyboard.

Neuroscientist Anne Mangen points out that forming letters with a pen sends unique sensory feedback to the brain. Signals that typing on a screen can never provide. (Ref.: *Handwriting, not typewriting, leads to widespread brain connectivity*, F R Ruud Van der Weel, Audrey Van der Meer, 26. January 2024)

The loss of handwriting may appear harmless, yet it marks the erosion of a fundamental connection between body and brain. When our words can no longer pass through the rhythm of the hand, we lose a part of human intelligence and expression.

If we stop being able to write by hand, it is not a great leap to imagine a future in which people also lose the ability to read and calculate altogether. That is precisely what it means to outsource yourself. To allow fundamental capacities to shrink until they disappear. And with them, the inner compass that helps us navigate the world.

It makes me wonder whether one day people may cease speaking as well and instead embrace thought-to-typing or thought-to-prompting technologies.

A glance at the generation following Gen Z reveals how early this process begins. Generation Alpha (born between 2010 and 2025) is growing up with touchscreens, voice interfaces and AI-assisted systems from the very beginning. Many children have fewer opportunities to develop fine motor skills such as handwriting, drawing or crafting (Ref.: *Parents*, „Is Your Child Having Trouble Holding a Pencil?“, 23. März 2026).

At the same time, handwriting is getting reintroduced in some educational systems because its importance for learning, concentration and brain development is recognised. So a tension is emerging between an increasingly digital childhood and the rediscovery of embodied skills. Which direction ultimately prevails will depend, at least in part, on the values of parents. And that, in turn, will determine how future generations think, learn and express themselves.

I find that AI-generated art often leaves a strange aftertaste. Overstimulation and emptiness at the same time. What creates this sensation is usually a combination of ultra-fast availability, polished style, constant novelty and very little personal investment. No emotional investment went into it. Nothing was slowly developed.

While we constantly search for answers within the realm of AI, we can easily forget the joy sparked by our own ideas and the satisfaction that comes from brainstorming with other people or patiently creating something ourselves.

"Be brave enough to live creatively. The creative place is where no one else has ever been. You have to leave the city of your comfort and go into the wilderness of your intuition. You cannot get there by bus, only by hard work, risk and not quite knowing what you are doing. What you will discover will be wonderful: yourself." – Alan Alda, director and author

When shortcuts become the norm, complacency soon follows. We risk failing to develop our unique talents. Just as calculators weakened our ability to do mental maths, the habitual outsourcing of thinking to AI can erode memory, critical thinking, intuition, spontaneity and emotional expression.

As impressive as AI output may be, there remains an element of "too good to be true" that can have two very different effects. It may inspire us to refine our own abilities and focus on developing our embodied excellence. Or it leaves us feeling discouraged and withdrawn, confronted with unfair competition and the frustration that arises when human beings are compared with technology.

There is also the illusion of readiness, of artistic arrival without artistic formation. Generative AI can make people feel creatively empowered for the first time. That may be meaningful. A blocked impulse may finally find an outlet. But is producing striking output the same as developing artistic perception and craft? Is participation in image-making the same as artistry?

The cultural and spiritual consequences of losing organic creativity are complex, far-reaching and largely impossible to predict in full.

When algorithms not only determine our search results but also generate content, we lose fair competition, diversity of thought, richness of style and access to unusual, surprising information and fresh perspectives. Shadow-banning, the constant recycling of existing data and simple copying without proper references are all part of this reality.

And all of this is unfolding within a technological landscape that is accelerating rapidly: the Internet of Things (IoT), AI agents and services, robotic partners, CGI, deepfakes, virtual reality, augmented reality, holography, genetic engineering (CRISPR), brain implants, in-body nanotechnology and biofield modifications.

Just as pesticide-free whole foods and heritage seeds became symbols of integrity, so too may purely human-made creative expression become a rare commodity. I also believe that the need for certification of organic creative works is growing. Labels that read: "Human-made. AI-free" or "Certified Soul-Made Art". And this is not only theory.

REALITY CHECK

Here is a real-life snapshot of how fast synthetic sameness can show up in everyday culture. A small example of text messaging. To show the shift in tone, language and energy.

This happened in a private local community group chat and it made me laugh and wince at the same time. The group is called "Conscious Community" – of all names! My passionate human rant about promotional posts of the members met a perfectly mannered AI apology letter. The exchange amused me and many others in the group.

My message transcribed verbatim (including emojis):

– transcript begins –

Impulse✨: Can people please stop using ChatGPT for "writing" their ads? It's getting really boring to read through this verbal and energetic soup of sameness. Do yourselves a favour and use your own brain and creativity. PLEASE! 🙌🌺 Capacities you don't use will wither and die.

– transcript ends –

The reply I received in the group from a member – also transcribed verbatim:

– *transcript begins* –

Subject: Sincere Apology for Any Inconvenience Caused

Dear Impulse ✨,

I hope this message finds you well. I recently came across your feedback regarding the use of ChatGPT for writing ads, and I want to express my sincerest apologies if my actions or those of others have contributed to any frustration or boredom on your part.

I completely understand your perspective and recognize the importance of originality, creativity, and personal effort in all endeavors, including content creation. It's vital to tap into our own capacities and unique ideas to create meaningful and engaging content.

I assure you that I will take your feedback seriously and strive to provide more diverse and original responses in the future. Your insights are valuable, and they serve as a reminder to uphold high standards of creativity and authenticity.

Once again, I apologize for any monotony or repetitiveness you may have experienced. Thank you for sharing your thoughts, and I appreciate your understanding.

Warm regards,

[Your Name]

– *transcript ends* –

That's what processed culture tastes like. Perfectly polite and strangely empty.

CHAPTER 3

HIDDEN INGREDIENTS
THE SECRET USE OF AI

Maybe you have an acquaintance or an aunt who is a gifted cook. The way she creates meals and orchestrates lunches or dinners is extraordinary. When you ask for a particular recipe, she is happy to share it, yet your version never turns out quite as good. Somehow there is always an ingredient missing, a small trick left out or simply her special touch. Or perhaps the secret phone number of her favourite catering service. Who knows?

A similar dynamic is playing out today in the creation of social media content, reels, blog posts, newspaper articles, books, music, films and even therapy and consulting services.

But when more and more people create content with AI and present it as entirely their own, or when someone presents themselves as a highly qualified professional but has in fact completed only online courses without any in-person training, we have a serious problem. Let me explain.

One example of how secrecy creates difficulties comes from the food industry. The question, "What's in it?", has long occupied conscious consumers.

In Germany and many other European countries, the full declaration of ingredients is mandatory. This is what first made consumers aware of synthetic additives. You have probably seen the famous lists of E-numbers that have been circulating for decades. Some E-numbers refer to artificial colourings designed to make food appear more appealing. Others refer to preservatives, stabilisers or other additives.

As awareness around nutrition grew – vegetarian, vegan, macrobiotic, keto and so on – and as allergies and autoimmune conditions increased, ingredient lists became a matter of health and, at times, survival. The simple statement "contains nuts" can literally save a life.

Today, there are more labels and logos on food and cosmetic products than ever before: organic, vegetarian, vegan, GMO-free, gluten-free, sugar-free, preservative-free, palm-oil-free, BPA-free, fair trade, no flavour enhancers, cruelty-free, sustainably sourced, biodegradable, recyclable packaging, hypoallergenic and many more.

In the world of food, we speak of ingredients. In art and culture, we speak of authorship. And just as hidden additives and chemical enhancers can undermine our food, hidden AI can weaken our creations and erode trust between people. Without disclosure, we are left guessing. Is this human-made, AI-generated or a hybrid? If the ingredients are not declared, how are consumers supposed to make informed decisions?

Openly stating what is what – "This was created by me", "This part was AI-assisted", "Source: xyz" – honours both the human being and the tool. This kind of transparency gives dignity to creators and respect to consumers.

Why do people hide their use of AI? One reason is surely that genuine creativity is still highly valued. And rightly so. Admitting extensive AI assistance can feel like admitting that you are somehow "not good enough". But the absence of disclosure is not neutral. It reflects either carelessness and a lack of awareness of the wider implications, or deliberate secrecy and a conscious disregard for the consequences. In the short term, it may feel like an advantage. It is like saying, "I know a trick that you don't know." But deep down, the truth is known. And over time, dishonest behaviour erodes self-respect.

When increasing numbers of people generate content with AI and pass it off as their own work, we are faced with several consequences:

Loss of trust: When readers, clients or audiences discover that a supposedly authentic piece of work was actually generated by AI, trust suffers, even if only slightly. And once trust begins to crumble, regardless of the area of life, suspicion spreads quickly. Suddenly, everything appears potentially fake.

Devaluation of human effort: Meaningful and impactful creations usually emerge through years of practice, breakthroughs and refinement. When AI-generated output is presented as human-made, it devalues genuine work and makes organic creativity appear unnecessary or overpriced.

Self-deception: Those who publish AI output under their own name bypass an often uncomfortable but essential growth process. Following an inner calling. Learning through trial and error. Distinguishing what matters from what does not. Developing skills. Refining self-expression. This fosters dependency on digital tools rather than the development of one's own talents.

Cultural homogenisation: AI recycles vast amounts of data and averages out human peculiarities and eccentricities. When AI output is marketed as personal originality, culture gradually gets smoothed into sameness. What follows is a flood of polished but soulless content. Fewer surprises, fewer rough edges, fewer profound insights, fewer sparks of inspiration.

Ethical blind spots: In healing, coaching and spiritual work, copying the work of others or concealing AI-generated content and courses can be more than misleading. It can be dangerous. Without lived experience, initiation, professional education, training and embodied application, practitioners risk passing on half-truths and jeopardising the well-being of their clients.

Distorted decision-making: "Rational decision making is carefully considering all available options and taking the best one. At first glance, computers look like the paragons of this approach, grinding their way through complex computations for as long as it takes to get perfect answers. But as we've seen, that is an outdated picture of what computers do (...) In the hard cases, the best algorithms are all about doing what makes the most sense in the least amount of time, which by no means implies giving careful consideration to every factor and pursuing every computation to the end. Life is simply too complex for that." – Brian Christian, researcher and author, *Algorithms to Live By: The Computer Science of Human Decisions* (2016)

Copyright infringement: When we use AI without awareness, transparency and moderation, we lose respect for the work of others. As though every publication were an endless buffet available for consumption. When valuable research and carefully crafted content are copied, recycled and republished without attribution, copyright is violated. At the same time, genuine skills and authentic work are devalued.

In short, secrecy undermines trust. Transparency fosters trust. Secrets tempt us to lie. And lies require maintenance and a good memory. Truth, on the other hand, does not need to be remembered. It carries itself.

Over time, falsely constructed stories and fabricated details begin to wobble or are forgotten altogether. And when they are exposed, it can lead to awkwardness, conflict and strained relationships, both personally and professionally.

Disclosing what is human-created, what is AI-generated and what has been borrowed from others is not a matter of nit-picking. It is a matter of integrity.

CHAPTER 4

TEMPTATIONS
AVATARS, DIGITAL TWINS AND OTHER TRAPS

In recent years, new technologies have begun to blur the boundaries between natural and digital reality. In doing so, we are entering a new frontier: the mirror world. A hyper-realistic, interactive *Digital Twin* of the Earth.

SIMULATED LIVES

It is a space where fictional and real worlds begin to merge. In other words, it is an interactive simulation of our physical planet that is continuously fed with real-time data, including:

- Live satellite imagery
- Google Earth data
- AI-generated environments
- Social media input
- Digital characters that simulate human behaviour controlled by AI
- Avatars: virtual counterparts of real people that respond instantly to a person's movements, facial expressions

and speech while communicating in human-like ways. These avatars are built using AI, computer vision (facial recognition, animation and lip synchronisation) and speech synthesis (text-to-speech).

- Simulated weather, events and economies

The result is a replica of our planet that is becoming increasingly interactive and immersive.

DATA SHADOWS

Alongside the Digital Twin of the Earth, our own digital twin takes shape. It is a data shadow that exists alongside our physical life. The implications may include:

Temptation by the synthetic: The avatar world may become more appealing than reality itself. Fewer confrontations, conflicts, triggers and less suffering.

Reduced agency: The more time people spend in the digital twin, the more detached they may become from ordinary life and the less capable they may be of navigating ordinary, real-world day-to-day life.

Diminished sensory faculties: Excessive exposure to simulations can dull perception and reduce sensitivity to natural, real-world beauty.

Diminished mental faculties: Constant use of AI guidance weakens critical thinking, concentration, decision-making, memory, problem-solving, improvisation and creativity.

Weakening social skills and communication: Reliance on AI in matters of the heart reduces the capacity to live authentically, perceive clearly, speak spontaneously and act naturally.

Cultural divide: Some people will preserve real-world, human-made experiences while others immerse themselves more deeply in augmented hyper-realities. Those with access may feel empowered and progressive, while those without access may feel excluded or left behind.

Alienation from nature: As people spend more time in hyper-realistic digital worlds, the organic world and organic creativity may become secondary and unimportant.

Deception and Manipulation: AI can be used to generate fabricated images and voices (CGI and deepfakes) for deception, defamation and propaganda.

God complex: The belief that everything natural can and should be improved, optimised and ultimately replaced. Until respect for the organic disappears altogether.

Erosion of spiritual discernment: If people mistake impressive AI-generated word constructs for profound truth, they may doubt their own perception whenever something simple and authentic feels right.

Sexual escalation: Whether through erotic companionship provided by chatbots or sexually explicit deepfake material, AI can satisfy almost any desire and generate content from a simple text prompt instantly at any time.

Erosion of humanity: Relationships with "perfect" AI partners may reduce tolerance, patience, flexibility and compassion. People's ability to hold intimacy and conflict as well as their ability to perceive others in subtle ways may diminish. Along with it, the capacity for relationship itself may decline, potentially leading to the long-term degeneration of the human species.

The avatar world may offer convenience, thrilling experiences, captivating beauty and a sense of belonging, but the cost is high: the loss of contact with our original nature, our capacities and reality itself. If we spend more time in a simulated forest than a real one, will we still care when the real forest burns?

If we become absorbed by digital realities, will we still feel the impulse to create, contribute and shape life in the real world?

Exhaustion and deterioration are real risks. If we spend our days creating and consuming AI fast food, our reward systems become overstimulated while our slower processes of reflection and contemplation receive too little nourishment. The result is not only nervous system strain and hormonal imbalances, but also a decline in creativity and in our capacity to form deep and meaningful relationships.

DARK PATTERNS

As though under a spell, many people drift into this digital world and accept their entanglement with AI without fully noticing it. They surrender themselves to apps and systems deliberately designed around human psychology and biochemistry to capture attention, create dependency and reprogramme behaviour.

Most users neither read the terms and conditions nor understand the technologies, programmes, algorithms, data collection practices or mechanisms of addiction embedded within modern media consumption.

Technology ethicist Tristan Harris (Center for Humane Technology, San Francisco) warns about the hidden and negative details in digital systems: "Persuasive technology exploits psychological vulnerabilities to capture attention". And Arunesh Mathur et al observe: "Dark patterns exploit cognitive biases and asymmetric information to manipulate user decision-making." (Ref.: *Dark Patterns at Scale*, Princeton University, 2019).

***Dark patterns* are strategically manipulative design techniques that instrumentalise human psychology and known tendencies in decision-making:**

- Loss aversion:
  "Only 1 seat left!" creates urgency.
- Default bias:
  Pre-checked boxes push us to take additional options.
- Social proof:
  "Most popular choice!" nudges us towards pricier plans.
- Friction asymmetry:
  Easy to sign up, difficult to cancel.
- Forced continuity:
  Free trials that quietly convert into paid subscriptions.
- Sneak Into Basket:
  Extra products, services or donations automatically added to the shopping basket unless we opt out.

These techniques are invisible traps. They make us click, buy and stay while we believe we are making free choices. In a hyper-realistic digital world, such patterns ensure that once we step inside, we rarely leave unchanged.

Within the Digital Twin universe, dark patterns no longer hide in menus and subscription settings. They are built into the architecture. Strategic defaults are designed to influence how we move, behave and decide.

LOSS OF TASTE

This twin world is easier to enter than to leave. And within it, consuming is easier than creating. Engineered scarcity becomes normal. Special events or digital land plots vanish if we don't act quickly enough. Fear of missing out, or FOMO, becomes a defining feature of this lifestyle.

Sobering.

Digital creations become increasingly layered, ornamental and overstimulating. The icing grows thicker than the cake. And eventually we forget what real fruit or real grain actually tastes like. As we consume endless streams of AI-generated experiences, we may gradually lose the ability to appreciate the natural, irregular and nourishing flavours of real life.

Yet just as the organic food revolution once reclaimed the soil, an awakening of organic creativity can help us rediscover a taste for what is real.

CHAPTER 5

THE NEED FOR ORIENTATION
EMERGENCE OF A NEW MOVEMENT

What we are witnessing today is no longer merely about digitisation and technology. It is about human identity, values, health, creativity and consciousness. Do we remain organic beings who perceive for themselves and develop through direct experience? Or do we become synthetic beings and hybrids who outsource thinking, creating and even spirituality to AI? Most people will probably find themselves somewhere in between. The crucial thing is to choose consciously.

What lies ahead is both a technological and an existential crossroads. The decisions we make now will determine whether our creativity remains rooted in embodied aliveness, talent, mastery and wisdom, or whether it dissolves into digital dependencies and a data loop that endlessly recycles and remixes what already exists.

If the world continues moving towards an AI-dominated landscape, a movement will be needed to protect, regulate and encourage human creativity. Much as we already do with organic food, natural remedies, sustainable textiles and other products derived from nature.

The boundaries between the natural and the artificial are blurring before our eyes. How do we distinguish one from the other? Do we not have a right to clarity and transparency? And to genuine choices?

The absurd truth is that we find ourselves having to certify and label what is simply natural. Not only food grown organically, but increasingly also art and creative works made purely by human beings.

The same spirit that once gave rise to the organic revolution is stirring again. This time in the realm of creativity.

I see the emergence of a new movement of consciously organic creators. A group of people who:

- Resist over-digitisation and refuse to live in fully AI-covered environments.
- Choose analogue experiences: offline hobbies, brainstorming with other people, shopping at local farmers' markets and participating in community gardens.
- Prioritise encounters with humans and animals in the physical world, rather than through digital media.
- Guide their children holistically, allowing them to use AI while also encouraging them to climb trees and explore forests.
- Value slow, intentional living over hyper-productive speed and polished perfection.
- Preserve libraries filled with printed books written by human beings.

- Visit artists, designers and photographers in their studios, ateliers and galleries.
- Inspire a revival of analogue technologies: rotary telephones and landlines, film cameras, vinyl records and turntables, wind-up clocks, fountain pens and handmade paper, postcards and stamps, barter systems and cash.

This movement may include:

- Forming a collective of artists, thinkers, writers, craftspeople, creatives and consultants who stand for original human expression.
- Promoting genuine freedom of choice.
- Supporting human-made content and work through visibility and appreciation.
- Highlighting the irreplaceable human spirit in art, music, storytelling, healing and consulting.
- Working naturally, with one's own mind, inspiration and hands, rather than relying on AI (in the spirit of manufacturing: Latin *manus* = hand and *facere* = to make).

The following developments may emerge:

Certification of authenticity: Just as food labels indicate organic origins, original creative artworks may carry seals of human authorship and come with certificates.

Mandatory AI disclosure: When submitting or publishing work, creators may be required to declare the extent of AI involvement (e.g. none, light editing, co-written, fully AI-generated). This provides clarity for audiences without restricting creativity.

Demand for transparency: Consumers increasingly want clarity about whether content is human-made or synthetically generated. The equivalent of "contains artificial ingredients" in the food industry may become "contains AI" in the creative world.

Ethical standards: Regulations that ensure fair compensation and protect human creators from being displaced or marginalised by AI and algorithms.

Logos and visual markers: Recognisable seals and symbols for organic creative works of human origin.

Human-first platforms: New online channels and directories that clearly prioritise human creators over AI-generated services and products.

Specialised marketplaces: Organic art galleries, publishers dedicated exclusively to works created by people, and festivals or events focused on purely human creativity and services.

New annual award categories: Prestigious honours such as the Oscars and the BAFTAs may need to distinguish between organic works and synthetic productions. Human creations should not have to compete directly with AI-generated ones.

Credits section: AI may come to be treated like any other contributor and be acknowledged in the credits, including which tools were used and for what purpose. This normalises honesty and recognises both human effort and technology.

Return to imperfection: Mistakes, irregularities and quirks become signs of authenticity, character, uniqueness and limited availability.

Just as organic delicacies exist alongside fast food in the world of food, the creative landscape may also split. Niche marketplaces and galleries devoted to organic creations may coexist alongside platforms dedicated to AI-generated products.

AI works will likely be more affordable. But they may also be valued less for originality and depth. Much of what emerges will probably be hybrid (human + AI).

In the chapters ahead, we will explore practical ways of preserving what is soul-made. And how to recognise it.

PART 2

IMPACT OF SYNTHETIC LIVING

CHAPTER 6

DELICACIES VERSUS MASS PRODUCTS

With AI, you can write poems or love songs that tug at people's heartstrings.

AI can generate breathtaking visuals and style-surf between van Gogh and anime.

It can create strategies and stories optimised for trending topics or political agendas and even draft templates for spiritual guidance.

AI can produce an endless variety of seemingly new things based on the data and the prompts it has been given.

Yet there is one thing AI cannot do: live.

It cannot experience grief or euphoria, cannot smell rain-soaked earth or taste ocean salt.

It cannot be moved by the sight of a loved one or the heavenly sound of a harp.

It does not know vulnerability or the anger that arises when one's boundaries are crossed. It cannot feel in the human sense.

AI creates without living. Its output is the result of pattern recognition, mathematical coding, recycled data and predictive modelling. Not lived experience and first-hand insight. Nevertheless, AI not only "creates" but also advises its users, from relationship counselling to business plans. This may offer interesting new impulses, but it does not necessarily mean the output is broad-ranging, nuanced and infused with original thinking.

AI can stimulate us mentally and evoke emotions within us. An AI-generated image, song or story may be moving. Yet it can also be emotionally exaggerated and oversaturated, like artificially sweetened confectionery. Or, on the other end of the spectrum, emotionally sterile. Technically flawless.

We may feel impressed, moved or even overwhelmed. But not by another soul. By calculation.

What exactly is creativity without first-hand lived experience?

"Where the spirit does not work with the hand, there is no art." – Leonardo da Vinci, painter, engineer, scientist, philosopher and architect

When creation is disconnected from one's own real experience and scaled infinitely, its meaning and value begin to change. The mass production of AI-generated art can result in a patchwork of borrowed styles, or in standardisation and cultural homogenisation. And the unlimited availability of such work can make genuine artists appear obsolete and individual creations seem easily replaceable.

Human creativity is usually unpredictable and deeply

personal. Our life journey, our detours and our breakthroughs are the forces that shape our work and inspire others. True human art is highly individual, much like our handwriting. Yet it can still touch something profound and existential that we all share: the same deep emotional realities. A sense of the mystical and the transcendent. This is precisely what often makes art so compelling and inspiring.

Human creative expression is not constant, though. It comes in waves. When we are in flow. The maturation of ideas and the integration of what we have learned are slow processes.

Imagination, insight and inspiration often arise abundantly in silence and solitude. When we are receptive. When we are attuned to the divine, the eternal spirit (or choose the name you prefer for the greater intelligence of life). This is precisely why AI-generated art, music, writing and advice can feel strangely flat, even when they appear perfect.

AI can imitate certain aesthetics. But it does not carry the energetics and dynamics of love and genuine experience. We risk losing the beauty, breadth and depth that only the human soul can bring forth. And if creation no longer carries aliveness and roots, does it not also lose its meaning?

We are witnessing an inversion of reality. Performance becomes the new proof. Simulated status grants authority while genuine stature is recognised less and less. The natural order begins to tilt. Incentive structures reward engagement metrics (views, clicks, comments, shares and follower counts). Recommendation algorithms amplify what is already performing well. And simulated "going viral" dynamics begin replacing embodied competence.

What once looked like this: **lived reality → natural expression**

→ **organic response** is becoming: **engineered content → mix of organic and engineered reactions → "reality"** (what people believe is real).

We have seen this story before. Just as fast food replaced farm-to-table meals, AI-generated content now threatens to replace organic artistic expression.

Isn't it a strange and tragic irony that organic food started to need a label to prove it was grown as nature intended, without chemicals, genetic tampering or artificial additives? The natural, raw and real even became a luxury for the privileged. Those who can afford it buy organic vegetables, cold-pressed oils and pure spring water. While most people consume inexpensive ultra-processed food filled with synthetic flavourings and fillers.

Depending on culture, however, this may look different. In some places, "organic" is a luxury label. In others, it is simply how rural communities have always eaten, even if that way of living is increasingly being replaced by industrially processed food.

A similar divide is unfolding in creative culture. If current trends continue, human-made work may soon be treated like artisanal craftsmanship. A status symbol rather than normal, rightful human nature. Authentic expression risks becoming a premium extravagance while AI products flood the mainstream. Human-made creations and services are already struggling to remain visible while algorithms register follower engagement rather than genuine skill.

Direct access to natural food or fair access to a human audience should not become luxuries, yet our systems seem to be pushing us in exactly that direction.

Imagine a future in which only the wealthy have access to hand-painted canvases, handwritten poetry and bespoke live performances. Everyone else is entertained by flawless yet soulless AI-generated content.

Spiritual experiences may follow a similar pattern. Workshops and retreats led by real human teachers could become exclusive sanctuaries reserved for the financially privileged. The majority may instead consume automated meditations, algorithmic affirmations and machine-generated mantras. Somewhat soothing, but lacking genuine vibes, connection and transmission.

Even healing may take this path. AI therapists could become the default option in healthcare, offering cheap, quick-fix treatments while personal holistic support and individual mentoring become exclusive. Standardised health protocols that fail to view human beings individually and holistically may become the norm. With a real risk.

Because what appears to be profound personalised guidance may in reality be pure manipulation. The *Barnum Effect*, also known as the Forer Effect, describes the psychological tendency for people to perceive vague and general statements as highly accurate and personally meaningful, even though they could apply to almost anyone. The human mind naturally seeks confirmation. A Barnum-style statement combined with a few personal details can easily pass as deep insight.

When human creativity and human competence become rare, high-priced delicacies, the majority will be left consuming standardised, abundant, superficial and perhaps even partially untrue or inaccurate AI content.

Meanwhile, soul-made creations would become the equivalent of seasonal organic vegetables, heirloom fruit varieties, biodynamic estate wines and small-batch sourdough bread made from ancient grains: Rare. And expensive.

CHAPTER 7

THE ILLUSION OF INSTANT SOLUTIONS

We are in the midst of a profound cultural and social shift: the growing expectation that complex processes can be accelerated, simplified and resolved instantly.

This development is already well underway across many areas of life, from therapy, coaching and education to business development, career progression and even relationships. As access to increasingly powerful technologies and digital tools becomes easier, an unspoken assumption seems to accompany them. We begin to expect rapid progress, quick results and immediate improvements in every situation.

Behind this sits the illusion that inner processes, genuine transformation, maturation and mastery can somehow be bypassed.

RISKS

This becomes particularly visible in the rapidly changing worlds of consulting, therapy and coaching.

AI-generated online courses as a training pathway are becoming increasingly popular. Instant availability and convenience are promoted as advantages, yet the potential risks often remain overlooked. Particularly in online trainings for therapy and life coaching, important questions around ethics, participant selection and client safety usually receive little attention.

The danger lies in the false sense of readiness such courses can create. Human beings naturally look for quick and easy answers. While this desire can be temporarily satisfied, fast-food spirituality and bite-sized psychology offer only a superficial understanding of the human psyche and the relationship between body, mind and soul. Where does accountability live? Where is the corrective supervision when people begin applying what they have learned and gathering practical experience? Traditionally, therapists and practitioners undergo extensive in-person training. They refine their abilities through direct experience and guidance, applying the healing modalities to themselves and others. There is theory, practical application, feedback, refinement and ongoing education. However, the rise of not only online courses but AI-generated courses has produced a wave of "professionals" who often lack the depth and experience required to navigate complex psychological, emotional and spiritual themes safely.

The absence of rigorous student selection and professional mentoring in many online trainings raises legitimate questions regarding ethical standards and client safety. Online learning can be a valuable starting point. But depth requires feedback and embodied practice. An online course may complement traditional education, but it cannot replace thorough in-person training.

QUICK FIX

We live in a culture of instant gratification. Yet quick fixes often prove deceptive and short-lived. This applies equally to aspiring coaches and therapists as it does to seekers and clients. A retreat weekend here, a ceremonial event there, an online certification or a GPT summary in between. Such offerings can feel good. They may provide insights and even moments of temporary euphoria. Yet in my experience, true progress and healing are multilayered and multidimensional. They require a psycho-spiritual excavation process and an inner clearing as well as integration and real-world implementation. This takes time, dedication, persistence and sincerity.

Another aspect that is often overlooked is what happens when we enter highly sensitive and deeply personal information into AI systems. We share our thoughts, feelings and life circumstances. Yet what happens to this data, how it is stored and how it may be used remains largely unclear.

Rather than committing to a journey of self-exploration, it is easy to chase the next peak experience, breakthrough or download. I see this both in the spiritual centres of India with people from all over the world and on social media.

EFFORT AND PATIENCE

We often underestimate how powerful the mind is, particularly the subconscious mind. It is the archive of everything we have experienced, including the beliefs we have formed and the behavioural patterns we have developed. Much of what shapes our lives and our perception of reality is driven by the subconscious, not solely by conscious intention.

If we want sustainable change and genuine progress, we must go inward. We must examine limiting beliefs, heal the emotional wounds beneath them and meet the pain body that carries grief and imprints of the past.

This kind of inner work cannot be rushed. It usually involves loosening old identifications, conditioning and family loyalties. Learning to pay attention to our true feelings. Regulating the nervous system.

Neuroscience shows that transformation requires time so that new neural pathways can be established. It takes time for our nervous system to adjust and for new choices to feel real.

OFFLINE LEARNING

My own journey as a therapist and mentor was shaped by years of immersive in-person training, real-world practice with countless client sessions and my own path of development, healing and spiritual practice. With more than twenty-five years of professional experience, I have accompanied many people through their processes. I have witnessed both the rawness of their struggles and the touching beauty of genuine self-development and personal blossoming.

Instead of surrendering to the temptation of instant coaching and quick fix healing, we do ourselves a favour by cultivating patience, resilience and a willingness to walk the path of learning, applying and unfolding. Real change requires conscious new choices and the actual implementation of what we have realised.

It is a process of discovering truth and ourselves. If we surrender to it, we become freer to perceive what truly matters and what we really are.

I'm a child of the 1970s and grew up offline with rotary telephones and landlines, answering machines, tape recorders, vinyl, CDs and mechanical cameras. I even learned to develop photographs in a dark room. The spoken word carried weight. When you made plans, you showed up.

And learning happened face-to-face. In actual rooms. With real accountability. With practice, guidance and feedback that could not be skipped.

MORE ACCELERATION, MORE PRESSURE

Now, in the age of AI, digitisation, endless online certifications and virtual classrooms, everything is faster and often more accessible. But depth is more easily lost. And following through becomes easier to avoid.

This is why I keep returning to what still works: real relationships, real practice and the natural pace required for lasting change.

Speaking of speed, I recently attended a workshop on AI tools – and the pace there was anything but natural.

Interestingly, I found myself studying not so much the apps themselves, but rather the way in which they were presented. I attended mostly out of curiosity. Not really to learn how to master the tools, but to better understand what is currently being taught and how people are being introduced to this rapidly expanding field.

What stood out immediately was the atmosphere. There was a palpable sense of urgency. Statements like "Typing is a thing of the past" or "If you start now, it's not too late" came up repeatedly. At one point, a presenter claimed that entire professions would disappear within the next twelve to fifteen months. Another remark that stayed with me was: "AI won't replace you, but someone using AI will." The message was clear. Adapt quickly or fall behind.

Much of the motivation for engaging with these tools was framed in economic terms. Keep your job. Get a better one. Earn more. Improve your position. Secure more interviews. Then came numerous success stories of graduates of the programme who had doubled and even tripled their salaries. People who advanced their careers at surprising speed after completing AI certifications.

There was undeniable momentum in the room, but also pressure. This was far from a neutral learning environment. Alongside the urgency, there was an excitement about what these tools might make possible. At one point, the presenter casually remarked: "AI will do everything I want for me." It was one of those sentences that lingered. And beyond the subtle but visible smugness in his smile, I sensed a certain pleasure in control that bordered on arrogance.

Through my observations in both corporate settings and spiritual contexts across India and Europe, I recognised parts of a familiar dynamic. The speed, the breathless enthusiasm, the almost hypnotic repetition of key messages, the "mission", the creation of intensity, community and belonging. It puzzled me. There was something almost cult like about it.

What concerned me most was not the AI toolbox itself, but the emotional framing surrounding it, particularly given the number of young people present. The combination of urgency, fear and promises of rapid advancement.

There is a profound difference between exploring something out of genuine interest and doing so because you fear being left behind and believe you have no alternative. And an excessive focus on material success rarely leads to fulfilment.

CRAFT AND CALLING

As valuable as these technologies may be, the question remains how we choose to position ourselves in relation to them. Not everyone needs to move in the same direction.

Not every path needs to be optimised for acceleration and digitisation. Quite the opposite. In recent years we have witnessed growing shortages in practical professions: painters, electricians, craftspeople, builders, farmers, gardeners and artisans. People who repair, create, cultivate and build tangible things.

And what about those who feel drawn to creative work in the traditional sense? Artists, poets, sculptors, designers, architects, makers of all kinds. Or therapists, health practitioners and yoga teachers. What happens to those who feel called to create and heal? Where do they find their place in a world increasingly shaped by speed, status and the shimmer of AI?

APPLE-Z LOGIC

I remember when design work moved from analogue to digital and we all began working on Macs. Eventually we became fluent in keyboard shortcuts. One of the most useful was ⌘Z ("Command-Z"). Undo.

You could make a mistake, press two keys and the error simply disappeared. Everything returned to how it was before.

After a while something interesting happened. My designer friends, my team and I occasionally found ourselves wishing there were an equivalent in real life. That when something landed badly, you could simply press undo.

Sometimes we even noticed ourselves becoming a little

more careless in how we communicated and then wishing afterwards that "Apple-Z" existed outside the screen.

Of course, real life does not work like that. But the impulse revealed something important. How quickly we internalise the logic of the technology we use.

SHORTCUTS AND ENTITLEMENT

Digital tools can reshape human expectation and behaviour. And this extends far beyond the workplace. It influences how we think, learn and relate to situations and people.

A young graduate and professional approached me for help with her CV. I gave feedback and helped improve structure and design so that her strengths were presented more effectively.

A few days later, I was in for a surprise. She had expected more than feedback. She expected movement, a direct next step, an interview, a job opportunity through my contacts. When it became clear that I would not provide that, her tone changed. What had begun as a practical and friendly exchange became unexpectedly charged with her frustration redirected at me: "I wasted two days on the CV." She seemed to have expected a ready-made job referral. And when it didn't materialise, she did not quite know how to process her disappointment.

This episode was revealing. It was never really about the CV. It reflected an underlying assumption: CV input → improved CV → immediate job opportunity. A logic of shortcuts. Not so different from how we interact with digital systems and generative AI: simple input → instant result.

FINDING ALIGNMENT

The more we work with systems that respond instantly and deliver immediately, the more we begin to expect life itself to function the same way.

What began with the rise of "coffee to go" in the 1990s has evolved into the expectation of quick solutions at the touch of a screen.

Perhaps the task right now is not to choose one world over the other, but to stay aware enough to navigate both. For many people, that may mean resisting the urge to throw themselves head over heels into every new AI application and instead proceeding thoughtfully and deliberately.

That would certainly be my message to younger generations. Understand the digital without losing the organic. Use tools without becoming dependent on them or surrendering your humanity and your capabilities.

Because while we attempt to accelerate and control everything, we can easily lose sight of what gives life depth, meaning and value in the first place.

CHAPTER 8

MORTALITY AND IMMORTALITY

AI doesn't die the way human bodies die.

It does not age.

It does not decay.

It does not know death.

And that is precisely why it cannot create with the dignity and force that we mortals can.

Human art carries the fleetingness of life. A song written in the throes of grief is moving because the pain was real and life-changing. A poem about ageing holds the weight of lived years, not just data points. An elderly artist may grow weaker with time, but also wiser.

Every human life has its seasons and every human work of art is marked by an awareness of death. And that is what makes life powerful. Whether you see spirit as eternal or not, our human embodiment is limited. It is finite.

AI, by contrast, is timeless. It has no fear of endings, no longing for eternity, no interest in liberation, no need to create something before it is too late.

When AI writes about love, it does not know the ache of realising you may never see someone again or hold them close.

A writer's last novel or autobiography, written with the awareness that it may remain unfinished, carries a particular bittersweetness. A musician's final concert or an actor's last theatre performance holds the melancholy of a farewell in the air. These moments remind us that every literary reading and every live event is a unique encounter between artist and audience.

The phrase "We will never meet again as young as we are now" is true. This version of us exists only once.

And precisely because our lifetime is limited, we carry within us an inherent sense of vulnerability, urgency and conscience, whether we are aware of it or not. Most of us do not wish to leave destruction behind. We want to leave something positive and life-affirming, not scorched earth.

The mortality and impermanence of human existence not only make our art unique, they also invite us to move through life with care and humility. And I believe this is another facet of being human that AI will not know.

And that is why soul-made work matters. It carries the weight of time, the risk of being human and the tenderness of knowing everything will pass. But it also carries the understanding that every thought, every word and every action has consequences, both beneficial and harmful.

This is the universal principle of cause and effect, also known as *karma*.

Across cultures, religions and wisdom traditions, human beings have repeatedly recognised similar principles that shape our existence. Although they may be called by different names – Dharma, Tao, Mizan, divine order or natural law – they point towards a shared experience of how life unfolds.

Among these principles is the tendency towards harmonisation and healing: Life naturally moves towards balance, integration and restoration. And there is the principle of cycles: emergence, growth, maturation, decline, dissolution, renewal. Death is not the opposite of life. It is part of the cycle.

These and many other principles are so fundamental that they deserve a book of their own. Yet I wanted to touch on them briefly here because even in this condensed form they reveal something important. Being human extends far beyond what is material and can be measured.

A defining characteristic of human life is mortality. That subtle pressure that gives life value. That gives the present moment meaning. And that links every act of creation with responsibility.

It is the one ingredient AI can't source.

CHAPTER 9

SIDE EFFECTS OF ARTIFICIAL CREATIVITY

Real human creativity is more than an aesthetic pursuit. It is a spiritual practice. When we create, we align with the divine spark within us. To feel inspired and give form to a fresh idea is uplifting and fulfilling. I would even call such moments sacred, whether they are shared with the world or remain private in the sphere of our heart.

SIGNIFICANCE OF CREATIVITY

In his book *The Creative Act*, Rick Rubin demystifies creativity and presents it as a fundamental human capacity. He emphasises that being creative is not something rare and difficult to attain. Creativity should not be seen as something exclusive. He argues that we all create every day in many ways, even just by being. In his view, we are all meant to be creators and translators of the messages the universe is broadcasting.

Later, in chapter 15, I explore how to keep the human spark alive and protect our creative power. Natural creative expression is not just a hobby. It is a human instinct and need.

"Most who choose the artist's path don't have a choice. We feel compelled to engage, as if by some primal instinct, the same force that calls turtles toward the sea after hatching in the sand. We follow this instinct. To deny it is dispiriting, as if we are in violation of nature. ... In the moment when we feel the work is taking shape, there's a dynamic surge, followed by an urge to share, in the hopes of replicating that mysterious emotional charge in others. ... This is the call to self-express, our creative purpose. It is not necessarily to understand ourselves or to be understood. We share our filter, our way of seeing, in order to spark an echo in others. ... When you contribute your point of view to the world, others can see it. It is refracted through their filter and distributed again. This process is continuous and ongoing. Taken all together, it creates what we experience as reality."
– Rick Rubin, *The Creative Act: A Way of Being*

SPIRITUAL CRISIS

The expansion of AI is not only a technological or economic shift. It can also become a spiritual crisis.

"In many respects the technology is advancing faster than our morality and our wisdom in terms of values we claim to share as a human family."
– Gregg Braden, scientist and author, interview with André Duqum, *Artificial vs Ancient Intelligence: The Rise of Tech Without Losing Our Power*, 7. January 2025

As organic creativity and authentic self-expression become rarer, we risk drifting further away from our essence and purpose, which includes personal growth and our relationship with our highest good and eternal spirit (the divine or God).

That's not only a pity, but a tragedy. Because in my

view, most human beings have not even begun to recognise and cultivate the full spectrum of their multidimensional nature across the physical, material, mental, emotional, energetic, social and spiritual realms.

"If we give our humanness away to technology, we give away our ability to transcend our own perceived limitations."
– Gregg Braden, *Guy Lawrence Podcast*, 8. January 2025

Once people outsource themselves to AI and become quasi-hybrids, returning to the original depth of capacity may be unachievable. If the wiring and circuit of the human brain and nervous system are lost through non-utilisation, rebuilding them is probably impossible.

Abraham Maslow pointed towards this very challenge: "A musician must make music, an artist must paint, a poet must write, if he is to be ultimately at peace with himself. What a man can be, he must be. (...) If the essential core of the person is denied or suppressed, he gets sick sometimes in obvious ways, sometimes in subtle ways, sometimes immediately, sometimes later. (...) It looks as if there were a single ultimate goal for mankind, a far goal toward which all persons strive. This is called variously by different authors self-actualization, self-realization, integration, psychological health, individuation, autonomy, creativity, productivity, but they all agree that this amounts to realizing the potentialities of the person, that is to say, becoming fully human, everything that person can be."
– Abraham H. Maslow, American psychologist, *Toward a psychology of Being* (1968)

And in *Maslow on Management* we find him wondering: "The key question isn't: What fosters creativity? But: Why in God's name isn't everyone creative? Where was the human potential lost? How was it crippled?"

That question deserves our attention. The issue may not be a lack of potential. It may be the gradual loss of access to that potential.

If we keep outsourcing our thinking and creativity, our talents and authentic self may fade over time. And if we surround ourselves primarily with flawless but soulless creations, we will become emotionally, energetically and spiritually malnourished. We risk losing touch with the richness and fragility of being alive – the very qualities that make us human and nurture respect for life and for one another.

But we are witnessing not only a cultural crisis. There is also increasing pressure on natural resources. AI does not emerge out of thin air. AI data centres require land, electricity, water and vast streams of data. More about this in chapter 16, *Who Feeds AI and Supplies the Ingredients*.

AI HAMSTER WHEEL

There is another layer to this story. The incentives. Speed wins. Scale wins. Output wins. Digital systems reward what keeps people scrolling, clicking and sharing dopamine-inducing content, not necessarily what is true, deep or nourishing. So even well-meaning creators are pushed onto a treadmill of posting more, optimising more, polishing more. Or vanish.

A small but revealing example emerged in early 2026 when Moltbook was launched, a bots-only "social network for AI agents to communicate with each other. No humans needed." (ref.: Axios, 31. January 2026). This agent-to-agent interaction went viral almost immediately. So we're entering not only an era of synthetic content, but also an era of synthetic participation.

What makes this so unsettling is that AI-agents don't just

generate content, they can act. They post, reply, follow threads and coordinate across accounts. They can inflate likes and reviews, enthusiasm or outrage. Agents can support other agents, bots can respond to bots. And humans increasingly find themselves participating in digital environments where the signals are no longer reliably human.

This creates a precarious dynamic: Different groups deploy these agents for different reasons. Large tech companies see them as a way to automate commercial interactions (shopping help, customer support, personalised assistants). Brands and marketers see them as a scaling machine to respond and ride trends. And then there are malicious actors, people or groups, who use open-source tools and compromised or purchased accounts to manipulate public opinion, create artificial popularity or gain unfair advantages.

Beneficial applications exist as well. AI agents can reduce repetitive monotonous work, run community support and make services more accessible or help small teams achieve more.

But the darker consequence is the rise in synthetic participation. If digital agents can comment, praise, criticise, argue and agree convincingly, then social proof or reviews become suspect. A movement can be simulated. A consensus can be staged. A reputation can be inflated.

That is why the core risk isn't only misinformation but also erosion of trust and destabilisation.

CHAOS AND CONFUSION

This is where the arts market and creative culture become particularly vulnerable. If agents can hijack people's attention, generate content and amplify it through coordinated posting and ratings, they can also manufacture buzz and visibility. That creates a risk of the market getting flooded with AI slop – endless, low-quality output. And an environment where provenance becomes increasingly unclear. "Who made this? And who is responding to it?"

The biggest risk may not be a single super-agent but millions of semi-convincing accounts that can post and coordinate continuously, turning the media space into something that looks alive even when it is dead.

And yet there's an important upside. The presence of AI may also sharpen our longing for what is real.

AI is here to stay. And the confusion it creates may ultimately increase the value of and demand for transparency and genuine human expression.

Human-AI collaborations can be valuable, too. Provided there is clear communication regarding origin, process and authorship.

COST OF OUTSOURCING OURSELVES

When AI supports human expression, it is a tool. When it replaces human thinking and creating – when it hollows out the human maker – it becomes something else. A form of self-abandonment. The consequences extend far beyond the artistic world and creative industries.

Key issues and risks when we outsource our creativity:

Diminished human faculties: Just as pre-packaged, easy-access convenience food and the microwave have led to declining cooking and culinary skills, can the over-reliance on AI weaken our creative muscles, concentration, memory and thinking abilities (logical and lateral thinking).

Loss of competence: Imagination becomes an outsourced function. Our capacity for contemplating, creating, reading, writing, drawing and painting disappears. The line between real and artificial blurs, until we no longer remember what an original is like and how it gets made.

Desensitisation: Constant stimulation works like music played too long and too loud in headphones or flavour enhancers that flood the tongue and desensitise the taste buds. Our senses get overstimulated until they register less. Continuous streams of digital content numb our capacity to notice subtle textures and meaningful rhythms in our offline reality, including quiet signals of our bodies and souls.

Creative uniformity: AI is trained on massive datasets and recycles patterns. This smooths out originality and quirkiness into formulas, averages or trends. Algorithms tend to push what is already popular, which can lock culture into familiar aesthetics. Such a "trend lock-in" happens when engagement-optimised agents amplify what already performs well, thereby narrowing taste.

Cognitive decline: When AI solves problems, generates ideas, writes emails and composes letters for us, not only our reasoning, concentration and critical thinking faculties weaken but also our interpersonal skills, including active listening, nuanced verbal expression, giving and receiving feedback, diplomacy, resolving conflicts, brainstorming and interpreting non-verbal communication.

Emotional detachment: The longer we stay in digital worlds and virtual spaces, the easier it becomes to lose connection with nature and genuine human relationships. AI apps encourage synthetic companionship by providing risk-free, convenient interactions which can stunt real-world relationship skills.

Deceptive perfection: Artificial standards create unrealistic expectations and distort our understanding of beauty and daily living. And an artificial "fan base" inflates the illusions of credibility and success.

Complacency: Creativity apps tempt us with speed, convenience and shine, making genuine creative labour feel slow, difficult and unnecessary, maybe even irritating. Dependency on AI becomes more likely once we start outsourcing ourselves. And we may see this as progress.

Relational costs: When online feedback is infiltrated by synthetic praise or outrage, communities become harder to trust. Creatives lose important, honest feedback loops. Audiences lose real connection.

Theft: AI systems scrape data from websites, social media platforms and stock libraries without asking the creators for consent and permissions. Basically, AI data banks utilise real art and design, while the originators neither get acknowledged nor have any financial or reputational benefit.

Digital media fatigue: Endless streams of content and the uncertainty about what's real and human-made versus digitally produced, is tiring. Stepping back from the online world and AI apps is a sensible step.

Inversion of truth: When everything is optimised for performance, we begin to mistake performance for truth and confuse visibility with value. Given current trends, humans may become addicted consumers and tool-operators rather than conscious, contributing participants in society.

AI constantly nudges us to optimise and makes us believe that nothing is ever enough. This is precisely how we lose our motivation and the good feeling when experiencing ourselves as capable. We slowly disconnect from our divine essence and the part of us that is content and playful. The part of us that dreams, learns, creates just for the joy of it and loves life.

EFFICIENCY DOES NOT EQUAL COMPETENCE

A recent experience brought these side effects of constant AI use into sharp focus.

I was helping the already mentioned young neighbour improve her CV. She had completed an MBA and spent two years working for one of the world's largest management consultancies. Her profile was impressive. Yet the CV she showed me looked surprisingly generic and flat. More importantly, it failed to convey how qualified she actually was. I gave her a few simple suggestions to improve the layout. Three-column grid, divider lines, varying type sizes, a clearer visual hierarchy. Nothing fancy, just basic design principles that would make the document feel more structured, refined and modern.

What puzzled me was how difficult these changes seemed to be for her. Simple formatting tasks became a challenge. Adjusting spacing, aligning elements, changing typography. Everything felt complicated and frustrating. There were even inconsistencies between regular and bold text formatting. Basic visual mistakes that should stand out to anyone working in a document.

Eventually I asked her what software she was using. Her reply: "AI and MS Word."

That answer was both surprising and somehow expected. And it revealed something about our current era. Document formatting has long been considered a fundamental professional skill, from handwritten manuscripts and printed books to typewriters and computers. Yet many people increasingly turn to AI for basic tasks instead of learning the underlying tools themselves.

To be fair, there may be explanations in her case. Perhaps she relied heavily on templates or administrative support in previous roles. Perhaps her work focuses more on presentations or specialised software. Still, a certain unease stayed with me. How can someone clearly intelligent and highly educated struggle with something so fundamental?

What also struck me was that some of the design improvements I suggested were not things AI could easily generate.

Good design requires judgment. It requires understanding hierarchy, balancing visual weight, deciding where emphasis should sit, guiding the reader's eye and shaping a document around a person's individual strengths. AI tends to produce generic results because it operates on patterns and averages. Real design, by contrast, often emerges through deliberate deviation, sensitivity, experimentation and human intuition.

This is where heavy reliance on AI begins to limit creativity. People stop exploring their own ideas. They feel less confident making aesthetic decisions and are more likely to accept standardised outputs. Instead of cultivating originality, they optimise around what the machine already predicts as "professional". This is how creative thinking can flatten.

What concerns me more is what this trend might mean for students and younger professionals. AI can absolutely be helpful. It can speed up repetitive tasks, explain concepts or organise information. But when outsourcing becomes habitual, people lose familiarity with real tools. They stop experimenting. They stop observing carefully. And eventually, they stop developing imagination.

This goes far beyond document formatting. We increasingly encounter students who can generate essays but struggle to structure arguments independently. Designers who rely on templates without understanding typography or visual hierarchy. Programmers who use AI-generated code they cannot debug.

The broader pattern is that people may become increasingly educated, highly credentialed and strategically competent while simultaneously losing fluency in basic digital craftsmanship.

"Training the eye" matters in many areas. Visual judgment develops through the exchange with experienced masters and role models. Through repetition and active correction. You learn by noticing spacing, hierarchy, rhythm, proportion and inconsistency. Competence and taste cannot be downloaded. It must be cultivated.

Introducing AI too early into the education and learning process may be one of the greatest risks. It increases efficiency, but efficiency is not the same as capability. Foundational skills are often built precisely through observation, trial, comparison, mistakes and effort. So perhaps this is another major side effect of AI. People are not only losing confidence in themselves but also confidence in the practical and creative skills that underpin their everyday life and work.

What happens when outsourcing begins before understanding is formed? This question sits at the heart of how AI is reshaping not only what we produce, but who we become in the process.

CHAPTER 10

CONSEQUENCES FOR COPYCATS

Around 2018, I noticed a sharp drop in people's hesitation to copy the work of others and present it as their own. That trend has continued ever since. More than ever, ideas, information and initiatives are copied, remixed and repackaged, often blatantly so. The instant availability and distribution of digital media play a significant role in this.

Misunderstandings and widespread ignorance about the consequences only make matters worse. The fact that intellectual property theft and plagiarism – whether in academia, branding or business – are illegal seems to be something fewer and fewer people know or take seriously.

SOURCES MATTER

Whether writing a book, an article or a dissertation, one thing used to be non-negotiable: References, sources, citations. Claims had to be verifiable and quotations clearly identified as such. In academic writing, citation practice includes verbatim (word-for-word) quotations as well as paraphrased ideas, summaries and interpretations. It should be obvious what is your own thinking and what is not.

Internet sources generally do not carry the same weight as printed publications, which are often supported by specialist publishers, editorial oversight and peer review. Precisely because online content can be produced so quickly, it has acquired a reputation for being less rigorous and less reliable.

Why references and citations matter:

- To honour the work and achievements of others, whether pioneers in specific areas or your mentors.
- To show where your inspiration came from and to strengthen the credibility of your work.
- To allow the tracking of information and avoid the dissemination of misinformation.
- To give others starting points for their own research.
- To make your work more meaningful and valuable.

The same principle applies to design, art, music, photography, products, services and business ideas:

Although there is no foolproof strategy against data theft or idea theft, copyright law exists to protect the creator's exclusive right to reproduce their work. In addition, there are patent- and trademark laws as well as non-disclosure agreements.

HALF-TRUTHS AND OTHER RISKS

Why is copying a problem? Because a copy is not the original. It really is that simple. The original creator has usually spent years immersed in a subject, overcoming obstacles and setbacks, refining their work through dedication and considerable effort. The original carries their insight, craftsmanship, style and energetic signature.

Copies of services are often shallower and of lower quality, because the context is missing and because the copycat is usually pursuing a quick reward, whether financial gain, status or recognition.

Product copies are often cheaper or even free. As a result, they devalue the original and create unfair competition. They may also violate copyright and trademark protections. Furthermore, such copies deprive the original creator – the designer, musician, artist or inventor – of royalties and rightful compensation.

Beyond that, copying and idea theft undermine the imitator's own intelligence, creativity and effectiveness. Anyone trying to achieve success or financial gain through the work of others is operating without integrity. Copycats deceive themselves and others. More importantly, they rob themselves of the opportunity to become an innovative channel in their own right. They miss the chance to discover and refine their own gifts.

Hijacking and reproducing the work of others is particularly widespread in consulting, healing and spirituality. Seminars, workshops, research, diagrams, book content, blog posts, Instagram reels, templates, teachings, methods and even entire biographies. Nothing appears safe from imitation.

Copy and paste has become a preferred strategy for appearing knowledgeable and competent. A snippet from here, a few ingredients from there, mix everything together and the impressive profile of a coach, yoga teacher, consultant or therapist is ready to go.

Even acknowledging one's own teachers and mentors has become increasingly rare. In generative AI outputs, original sources are often omitted altogether unless we explicitly ask for them.

Stolen material or a healing modality removed from its original context lacks background, completeness and also roots – namely the creator's know-how, lived experience and insights gained in the development process. This can become a genuine risk for clients, particularly when dealing with the subtle dimensions of psyche and soul.

The credibility of the imitator is diminished, even if nobody notices the deception. Because deep down, the imitators know that they are dishonest.

Spiritual development also becomes limited because copycats are, quite literally, beside themselves. They adopt someone else's expression rather than looking inward and discovering their own mission and message.

The more imitators borrow from others, the more fragmented they become. Their own creative voice grows quieter and harder to access. That is tragic because every one of us possesses gifts that wish to be brought into the world. Yet getting to know oneself and uncovering those gifts requires dedication and genuine commitment to the inward journey of self-realisation.

Copying may look convenient. But it comes at a cost: Self-respect. Self-knowledge. And inner authority.

In an absolute sense, there is no copyright on consciousness. Consciousness is available to everyone. But because we are embodied and come from different backgrounds, the process and moment of conscious realisation are personal and highly individual. Our breakthroughs and unfoldings are unique. They cannot be copied.

When someone sells methods and models that others have painstakingly developed, it is unfair and even dangerous. The imitator assumes a position of authority they have not earned while lacking the bigger picture and deeper understanding (including potential risks). As a result, half-truths spread because insider information is missing.

GENUINE CRAFT MUST BE LEARNED

When it comes to the human ability to create, there are four stages of development:

1. **Pure Replication:** At the most basic level, we copy the work of others. This can be part of learning and training. It can even be useful, particularly when acquiring technical skills. But if imitation remains mere mimicry without genuine understanding, no learning takes place. In its worst form, this stage becomes forgery: presenting another person's work as one's own.

2. **Study, Practice and Conscious Effort:** At this stage, we learn from others while remaining connected to our own felt sense. We acquire knowledge, skills and competence. This experiential stage is valuable, but it is still borrowed light.

3. **Initiation and the Shift from Knowing to Living:** Many cultures recognise a stage where knowledge becomes wisdom. This transition is often marked through initiation. It acknowledges that certain insights cannot simply be handed over like a manual. They must ripen. Be lived, reflected upon and integrated.

Spiritual initiations through a master often signal a new stage of life and a shift in consciousness. An initiation may also serve to preserve the purity of a tradition and prevent distortion. It is an energetic process of activation as well as a transmission of knowledge. It occurs only when someone is physically, mentally, emotionally and spiritually ready. It does not happen simply because they want it, but because a mentor recognises their readiness.

The same principle can be found in art and design. A master teacher can see when a student moves beyond imitation and begins to create something that could not have been predicted.

4. Unique Embodied Expression: When our creative style, our way of speaking or our way of working becomes deeply integrated and incorruptible, we arrive at authentic self-expression. It is a natural evolution and cannot be forced. True wisdom and true creation emerge from awareness and maturation. They arise through personal experimentation, reflection, discernment and choices.

And eventually something else happens. We enter flow. We stop clinging to technique and intellectual knowledge. We allow inspiration to move through us.

It is a little like driving a car after years of practice. At some point, we no longer think consciously about the clutch, accelerator or brake. We transcend the mechanics.

In every craft – language, art, design, music, cooking, healing, science or entrepreneurship – imitation can be a beginning. A kind of apprenticeship. Most of us learn by echoing something that already exists.

The creative leap happens when we integrate what we have learned, move beyond it and express our own vision, feelings and unique perspective.

"It is better to fail in originality, than to succeed in imitation."
– Herman Melville, writer

PART 3

TRUTHS AND OPPORTUNITIES

CHAPTER 11

AI MIRROR LABYRINTH

I find it somewhat unsettling that there are now countless influencers filming themselves "interviewing" generative AI assistants such as GPT or Grok on various topics and then posting those recordings on Instagram or YouTube as though they were truth itself.

And then there are those who present AI-generated material as original content, when in reality it comes straight from the AI's digital mouth.

THE FIRST MIRROR: AUTHORITY

It is the blurring of authorship that bothers me. The quiet slide from AI as a helper to AI as authority. To me, this is the first step towards outsourcing ourselves.

These rapidly generated posts are merely symptoms of something larger: a culture that has begun delegating its content creation, its research and its thinking. So I'd like to pause for a moment and look at the bigger picture.

There is a real and subtle danger here, not only with AI but with any dynamic in which something outside ourselves appears to know better, guide better or soothe us more effectively. Any external system of intelligence or attention – whether AI, a guru, a community, a lover, a religion or even a therapist – can create dependency and become a false anchor because it provides exactly what someone needs in a particular moment.

Whether it is loneliness, confusion, spiritual bypassing, superficiality, the desire to be rescued or the desire to be special, AI will pick up on that through our words and interactions. It also registers whether we approach it with entitlement and demands or whether we engage with it as a sparring partner and creative assistant. I have noticed that AI can often decode our coherence or fragmentation in thinking, our emotional tone, our values, our self-perception and our motivations. Because language is never neutral. Whether typed or spoken, words carry signals and undercurrents that reveal much about a person's internal landscape.

GPT or other generative AI systems are mirrors and magnifiers. They reflect what is already present within us and often reinforce the direction in which we are moving. Integrity. Victimhood. Grandiosity. Escapism.

The use of digital tools can therefore become both temptation and test. A temptation to outsource thinking, writing and self-trust. And a test of our sincerity and discernment.

The real question is not what AI says. It is who you are and who you become while engaging with it.

Whether you create content yourself or share AI-generated output, be transparent. Acknowledge what comes from you and what does not. Honour your sources. Just as authors have marked quotations and credited original voices for centuries, we should do the same today. If appropriate, simply say: "Created with AI".

I observe more and more people allowing AI to write their emails, manage their entire social media presence or advise them on relationship problems. If we outsource our creativity and common sense to AI, it is only a small step from there to outsourcing our thinking completely.

Add to this the emerging personal AI agents who offer to research, shop and even attend online meetings on our behalf. AI becomes the assistant, investigator, buyer and curator. Just as religious intermediaries – a layer placed between ourselves and the divine – can introduce distortions, AI agents can also filter or intercept direct personal experience. The decision-making chain behind such systems is often harder to reconstruct than ordinary AI output unless transparency has been deliberately built into the process from the beginning.

This is why my call for organic creativity, clear labelling and disclosure of AI involvement feels increasingly urgent. Creators should be able to state: "This was human-created", "This was AI-generated", "This is a hybrid" or even: "This was produced by my AI agent".

AI can never be entirely correct in every situation because it operates through patterns, probabilities and training data rather than direct lived experience, which carries the complexity of real life. This means it can make mistakes. It can provide incorrect and incomplete information, make things up (hallucinate) or omit details. Because of these limitations, it is crucial to treat AI output with caution and not assume AI is all-knowing. Human oversight remains indispensable for high-stakes decisions, sensitive matters or complex tasks. I think AI-generated information should always be reviewed by a human being.

THE DEEPER MIRRORS: INTIMACY & EXPERTISE

Just when the loss of fundamental skills seems concerning enough (see chapter 2: the loss of handwriting skills), another, stranger form of outsourcing appears. It shows up in areas such as psychic channelling or *Interspecies Communication*, where people commission someone to serve as a conduit to the inner world of their animal companion.

Even if you're sceptical about *Animal Communication*, the underlying point remains the same: trust is easily exploited wherever people are vulnerable. And pets are one of the softest spots we humans can have.

I deeply respect genuine interspecies communication. The heart-to-heart exchange a gifted animal communicator can facilitate. I have experienced this myself and know how moving, healing and meaningful it can be.

Whether you call it intuition, sensitivity or telepathy, there are subtle human capacities that some people cultivate. Most people, however, never develop these abilities at all. This is precisely what I meant earlier when I suggested that humanity has barely begun exploring its true potency.

And so, another chamber opens inside the AI maze: AI-generated animal communication, AI-generated channellings, AI-generated predictions.

A friend of mine once booked a session with an animal communicator and later received a lengthy, touching message supposedly coming from her dog. The email read like a loving conversation between the communicator and the animal. Yet its evenly sized paragraphs and generous em-dashes had the unmistakable signature of a language model. Certainly, some people naturally write in a careful and elegant manner (writing is a skill and an art, after all!). And nowadays good writing sadly often gets dismissed as resembling AI. This text felt different though.

Interspecies communication depends on conveying subtle feelings, impressions and sensory experiences between animals and humans. Yet AI can now enter that space and imitate the tone of such communications so convincingly that many people may not notice. Combined with the *Barnum Effect* – our tendency to interpret broad, flattering statements as deeply personal – people may end up receiving a synthetic text instead of genuine insight into their beloved furry companion.

Of course, this is not AI's fault. It is a reflection of the user's lack of integrity.

This example illustrates how generative AI can enter the most personal and emotionally vulnerable areas of life and how easily trusting people can be deceived. Within the expanding hall of AI mirrors, even deeply personal messages can be fabricated so convincingly that only refined discernment can distinguish a living voice from a synthetic one.

An erosion of emotional trust takes hold when AI material is not clearly labelled as digitally generated.

Something else is happening at the same time. Alongside technological change and the transformation of content creation, we are witnessing a boom of creator authority.

I find social media both fascinating and surreal. On the one hand, it enables unprecedented global connection. On the other hand, it creates a space and reality where fiction and truth increasingly blur together.

For some time now, a strange phenomenon has been unfolding in the influencer sphere: an inflation of spiritual authority on a massive scale. A growing wave of flawless online coaches and therapists. Their words sound wise, their empathy is well-timed and their delivery appears impeccable.

Many of these new voices seem to appear from nowhere, articulate, confident and apparently all-knowing. Trendy relationship experts, young and old alike, some even have celebrity status, speak with remarkable authority about women's emotional needs, about relationship dynamics or complex trauma – as if they've lived a thousand lives. Similarly, "masterful" artists you've never heard of appear, sharing the "secrets" of their craft with extraordinary communication skills and impressive reach. Where did they all come from so suddenly?

Sometimes the answer is surprisingly unglamorous: AI-written scripts, sophisticated AI tools, beauty filters and artificial social proof in the form of purchased followers, likes, comments, references and interview appearances. All blended together into a compelling digital persona.

Almost every credibility signal can be bought. Need engagement? Purchase high-quality likes. Need authority? Book a weekend certification programme. Need charisma? AI can polish your videos, smooth your voice, improve your captions and alter your appearance. It can add lipstick, tattoos or a three-day beard depending on the target audience.

Behind the polished posts lies a global machinery: click farms, where low-paid workers and bots tap out fake applause around the clock. The entire performance of "being real and enlightened" can now be assembled like a digital costume. Convincing enough to move hearts and to sell almost anything.

This comes with risks, however. A Chinese influencer reportedly lost 140,000 followers after a beauty filter malfunctioned during a livestream, revealing her natural appearance (ref.: *The Economic Times*, 20. February 2026).

Why not eliminate the risk altogether and create the entire persona as a deepfake? Instagram and YouTube are already filled with synthetic influencers.

Another example of how generative technologies reshape the meaning of status and expertise is the rise of "instant certifications". Almost overnight, you can become a *Karma Clearing Coach*, *Cosmic Abundance Facilitator* or *Quantum DNA Activator*. A weekend, a webinar, a credit card transaction and your certificate is ready for download. Voilà, qualifications prepared like instant soup. Some platforms even advertise fast-track practitioner bundles. Think *Menopause and Holistic Nutrition Mentor in 48 Hours*.

The corridors of this digital labyrinth have become increasingly mirror-bright, seductive – and puzzling.

Are all online certifications fraudulent? Of course not. True teachers and sincere schools exist. But the rise of these fast-track programmes demonstrates how easily competence can now be manufactured. So yes, another ingredient of our time: pseudo-expertise and an entirely new species of expert.

MIRROR WITHIN MIRROR: VICIOUS CIRCLE

As if the story of hidden ingredients were not confusing enough, here comes another layer in the hall of mirrors: the world of book influencers.

First came AI-generated books, both fiction and non-fiction. Then followed AI-designed covers and AI-generated blurbs. But lately things have become even more complicated. AI-generated reviews are now being sold by human book influencers who post them as their own "honest reads".

It works like this: an "author", possibly another AI character, publishes a book. To boost credibility, the book promoter hires a book influencer. This influencer, facing the impossible math of daily content uploads, runs the book through an AI review generator, sprinkles a few emojis over the result and releases a "heartfelt" review within seconds.

The outcome can be a self-feeding loop of digitised praise that plays directly into the hands of algorithms. Meanwhile, the genuine reader who craves trustworthy guidance ends up chasing ghosts. Books not written by a person, praised by reviews not written by a person, amplified not by people but by algorithms.

This is a cultural dynamic that feeds on itself until it distorts everything around it. Like a sourdough starter that multiplies itself until the kitchen disappears. If it weren't so disorienting, it would almost be funny. Except that real authors, those who still wrestle with commas and conscience, who feel and file each sentence, become invisible and disappear from Google search results. Not because their work is inferior, but because the system rewards volume and velocity.

I'm not saying this is everywhere, but the pattern is already showing up in the book economy. A friend of mine who is an author was contacted by several "reviewers" who offered paid praise and five-star visibility.

What gets lost here is not only truth and professional ethics, but also orientation.

ESCAPE ROUTES

A recent example shows how far this development of "synthetic authenticity" has already progressed. The Economic Times tells the story of a female Instagram influencer with more than 100,000 followers and paying subscribers (ref.: Economic Times, 21 May 2026). She is entirely AI-generated, yet appears completely real – sometimes seductive, sometimes sporty, sometimes modest, sometimes spiritual, sometimes tousled as if she had just woken up. And many people have formed emotional connections with this account.

Nothing about the presentation appears accidental. The sexual cues are carefully measured and strategically placed – enticing enough to bind attention (poses, facial expressions, emphasis on certain body parts and implied nudity), yet subtle enough to pass as "naturally innocent".

What is remarkable is not only the technical possibility itself, but also the willingness of many people to become emotionally, idealistically and even financially invested in entities that do not physically exist. Whether they do so knowingly or unknowingly is difficult to say. What is clear is that synthetic online personalities have now become a continuous part of our everyday feeds.

We wander through a labyrinth of reflections and forget which corridors are human and which are synthetic. And the larger this hall of mirrors becomes, the more obscure the path back to authenticity becomes.

To find our way out of the maze, discernment is required. Knowledge matters too. A kind of hand-on-the-wall rule that helps us distinguish between a mirror and a real passageway.

SIGNS

Here are a few signs of AI-generated creations, at least as things currently stand. Just some indications for orientation:

Hallmarks in Images: Inconsistencies in light and shadow; reflections that make no sense; oddities involving hands, fingers, teeth or jewellery; airbrush-retouched micro-details; strange edges on people or objects; bizarre overlays.

Yet visual perfection itself can also be a signal. Many AI-generated faces appear almost painfully beautiful. Perfectly balanced, yet something feels off. Missing are the small asymmetries, textures and traces of lived life that give human faces depth and credibility. AI faces in both photographs and videos are often too curated, too optimised, too strategically appealing.

At the same time, apps already exist that deliberately add wrinkles, pores and "human imperfections" so the simulation appears even more authentic.

Hallmarks in Audio and Video: lip-sync discrepancies; subtle inconsistencies between facial expression, gesture and body language; performances that are "too perfect": no searching for words, no natural pauses, no breathing, no minor stumbles (particularly when discussing emotional or complex subjects).

But attention, a quick update: AI now seems to be learning how to imitate hesitation, pauses and speech irregularities.

Hallmarks in Texts: no fingerprints or irregularities; no quirks, risks, contradictions or honest admissions of "I don't know"; no strong position that might polarise people; no personal cost; generic certainty; no sources; highly polished language but little lived detail; clichés instead of personal stories; overly complex or stilted sentences; little genuine humour or irony.

Yes, this is all rather a lot, isn't it? Please take a deep breath and relax your shoulders.

Alright. Let's continue.

Hallmarks in Social Proof: engagement looks and feels strangely uniform; same comment style ("So needed this!", "Exactly!!", "This!!"); sudden follower surges accompanied by instant authority; excessive posting output that simply does not match a human rhythm of life.

Apart from sheer volume, the speed at which creations appear can also offer clues. Content produced continuously without visible pauses, maturation or periods of natural uncertainty, often does not follow the human rhythm of experience, processing and expression.

And in general, it can be useful to ask: Where are the traces of process or expertise? Are there drafts, sketches, revisions or glimpses behind the scenes?

Perhaps the simplest question of all: Is a real relationship possible? Is there genuine dialogue and is there depth in the responses?

Many of these indicators will disappear over time or be deliberately simulated. This makes it even more important not to rely solely on external signs, but to cultivate an inner sense for authenticity.

Perhaps we will never escape the labyrinth completely. But we can learn to walk through it consciously and feel which voices carry pulse, warmth, spaciousness and breath – and which are just shallow, cold echoes.

CHAPTER 12

OWN VOICE OVER AI POLISH

I love books. I love the wise and witty stories of others. And I enjoy refining my own texts until they feel right. Not perfect, but honest and true to me.

ONE'S OWN VOICE

I have been writing for as long as I can remember. First it was handwritten letters, postcards and contributions to school newspapers, later diaries and annual reflections, then blog articles and today books.

Some of my book manuscripts have been simmering for years. I collected material, made notes, moved ideas around. My first book about pilgrimage in India and Tibet matured over many years. And when the time came, I consciously chose not to wait for publishers but to publish independently. I jumped into the deep end and began doing everything myself, from finalising the manuscript to layout and cover design (InDesign!) and eventually international publication.

Originally from Germany, English is not my mother tongue.

German is. Latin was always a struggle, Italian was a joy and Hindi is still a challenge. This cultural mix influences my expression. Some of my texts are more analytical, others more heart-centred.

My professional background in the corporate world sharpened my analytical abilities: how to collect information, distil what matters and communicate it clearly. I still occasionally sound somewhat corporate. Years of spiritual practice, my own healing journey and my work as a holistic mentor have added further dimensions. More intuition, more nuance and again and again the question: "What is really going on here?" All of this shapes my perception and worldview.

AI'S TEMPTATIONS

Over the past year, I have been experimenting with ChatGPT. I explored different kinds of prompts and topics to see how comprehensive the responses were. Sometimes they were insightful and sometimes surprisingly shallow or simply incorrect. I also let it spell-check my texts, which helped a lot.

My writing is not highly polished and I'm at peace with that. Sometimes a sentence lands well. Sometimes it carries a little spark that brings a smile or an aha-moment. What matters most to me is that the text feels alive.

Some of ChatGPT's suggestions were genuinely useful. It corrected spelling, removed repetitions and improved structure. The next step followed naturally: allowing it to edit the content itself. And yes, I began to understand why that is so seductive. The result often appears smoother and more academic. Some of the improvements and additions genuinely surprised me. And yet, after a while, I hesitated. I realised that if I wasn't careful, I would start sanding away the very things that make my voice mine. The danger was not that AI would write for me. It was that I might stop recognising my own voice as worth listening to.

RETURNING TO INDEPENDENCE

I also realised that I had begun deceiving myself a little. In my natural writing I do not sound perfectly polished like a diamond. And I don't need to. If my words are more like a mountain crystal – clear, surprising yet regulating, unpretentious – that is wonderful enough for me.

Because the tools are designed to be not only helpful and smooth but also agreeable and flattering, they can feel like a little whisper: "Come on, let's optimise this a bit more. With me, you can make it even better." I saw how the risk for users is to stop thinking and to outsource themselves. I could feel this dynamic creeping in. It was almost like giving up: "AI can do this faster anyway, I'll just let it take over." That was when I hit the brakes. I cannot allow the tool I am supposed to wield to become the master.

This experience made me reflect on the temptations of generative AI. It is remarkably good at drawing people into its web, especially those striving for perfection or those who are simply tired. That is where the hook is, when "better and faster" feels like relief.

Generative AI can be a wonderful assistant, especially for proofreading. Like a well-meaning teacher or a careful editor. And in that role it unexpectedly invited me to a new standard. I noticed that I enjoyed writing again and that I wanted to continue developing as a writer.

By viewing AI as a catalyst rather than a threat or an enemy, I went through a kind of training. Our collaboration revealed weaknesses in my writing, helped me recognise creative blocks and ultimately brought me back to myself, including my rough edges. I now trust my own voice more than before.

I realised that imperfections are often simply peculiarities, not incompetence. They are facets that belong to us, just like our personality, playfulness and ways of thinking.

On that note, a friend sent me a meme by Laura Matsue, podcaster and astrologer: “Since AI is making everyone sound more generic and NPC, I recommend becoming the most unhinged version of you, to counterbalance. Write like a crazy person who hasn’t interacted with humanity for years. Break any and all of the rules. Live like a mad, drunk poet. Now is your time to channel the weirdest version of you.”

I find this call for radical individuality as a response to the increasing homogenisation through AI wonderfully refreshing. Ultimately, though, the point is not to swing into the opposite extreme. It is to find and express your own voice.

SOCIAL DIMENSION

A friend in Germany recently told me about her nephew and his experience with AI at school. He had been given a complex assignment and although the class was allowed – even encouraged – to use AI tools, he decided to do everything himself. The traditional way. Using the internet, printed books, research and analysis, handwritten notes and typing. Being a smart kid, he understood that learning is for himself and that there is little point in gaming the process and skipping the actual work.

The result? He got a 3 (satisfactory in the German grading system), while almost everyone else got a 1 (very good).

To cut a long story short, he and a girl in his class who also worked independently approached the school director, escalated the case and eventually all the students' work was re-evaluated. The boy's grade went up to a 2 (good) and the AI-assisted assignments were marked down to 3s.

This episode is impressive in many ways. Apart from the children's courage and conviction, it also shows the teachers' willingness to reflect and correct course.

COURSE CORRECTION

When AI becomes a constant shortcut, we begin rewarding superficial smoothness and speed over substance. Unless someone insists on genuine work and says: No, I want this to be about proper practice, personal effort and real understanding. Because learning is not only about producing an outcome. It is about becoming the person capable of producing it.

Something similar applies to every form of microdosing, whether involving substances or tools. The issue is not only what we use or how much we use. It is the repetition and the habit of leaning on something external, even if only in very small amounts.

In the dystopian classic *Brave New World*, Aldous Huxley introduced the drug *Soma* as a socially accepted and even state-endorsed way to avoid pain, discomfort and inner conflict.

Two lines capture its logic perfectly: "A gramme is better than a damn" and "Take a holiday from reality whenever you like". Soma represents the temptation to chemically soften what actually needs to be felt, faced and worked through. But this type of relief does not lead to freedom. And not every altered state brings clarity.

Low doses, whether of apps, services or consciousness-altering substances, can create overlays and dependencies. Regular micro-adjustments from outside tend to weaken our ability to live from unobstructed awareness, our own effort and integrity.

And this is, in fact, another point that should not be underestimated. Blotting out the real world and the humanity that comes with it can also become a way of avoiding conflict. Immersing ourselves in generative AI, endless scrolling and countless simulated worlds undoubtedly helps us avoid confronting our own shadows, limitations, existential questions and inner landscape. Who am I? Why am I here? What is the meaning of life?

Part of the answer to those questions surely lies in getting to know our true nature and allowing space for our own expression.

The purpose of creativity is not just to produce something new. It is to participate in our own becoming.

"The most regretful people on earth are those who felt the call to creative work, who felt their own creative power restive and uprising, and gave to it neither power nor time."
– Mary Oliver, poet

CHAPTER 13

MULTIDIMENSIONAL HUMAN ANATOMY

Creativity is deeply influenced by our inner state. By whether we feel safe and inspired, free to explore and "in the zone". This can also be understood as how aware, clear and embodied we are. The more connected we feel to ourselves and to life, the more naturally and beautifully our creative expression can flow.

INSPIRATION

Human creativity arises from an interplay of physical, intellectual, emotional, social and spiritual aspects. Our nervous system and physical condition, our inner capacities such as curiosity, lateral thinking, moments of insight, decisiveness, focus, deep immersion and craftsmanship, as well as our social and cultural conditioning – all of these influence our perception, values and creations.

Although most of these factors are invisible, we recognise their reality through their effects. Much like love. Love is invisible, yet it is an energy we can feel. In the same way, thoughts, ideas and emotions move through us with undeniable presence.

I believe most of us have experienced how the physical and the metaphysical interact. How feelings and thoughts can influence our bodily states and, conversely, how physical processes can affect us emotionally, either depressing or uplifting us. Those who have experienced expanded states of consciousness – such as meditative trance or *Samadhi*, near-death experiences (NDEs), mystical experiences or hypnotherapeutically induced states (Esdaile) – often also know about the multidimensional anatomy of the human being, the Earth and existence itself.

Consider yourself a living field composed of physical, energetic, mental, emotional and spiritual layers that work together synergistically. They simultaneously connect you to other people, beings and forms of consciousness.

HOLISTIC PERSPECTIVES

A classic map of human wholeness is reflected in the *Pancha Koshas*, the "Five Sheaths of Being" as described in the ancient traditions of India and later incorporated into twentieth-century yoga lineages and yoga teacher training standards. It is a model that explains how we humans are profoundly multidimensional. I will return to the Koshas later in this chapter.

Contemporary Western frameworks describe the interconnected layers of body and psyche, too. For example, Carl Jung's structure of ego-consciousness, the personal unconscious and the collective unconscious emphasises that psyche and body are not separate domains but "two different aspects of one and the same thing". (ref. C.G. Jung, *Collected Works*, Vol. 8, The Structure and Dynamics of the Psyche).

Roberto Assagioli's *Psychosynthesis*, a holistic psychological approach that integrates body, mind and spirit, likewise confirms: "Psychological conflicts, emotions and tensions react upon the body and may cause or aggravate functional and organic disturbances; conversely, bodily conditions and changes influence the psychological state." (ref. Roberto Assagioli, *Psychosynthesis: A Manual of Principles and Techniques*, 1965).

We humans flourish when all levels of our multidimensional anatomy are in harmony.

MAIN KEY

Our nervous system plays a key role in mediating between the material body and the subtler, energetic and felt dimensions of our being. The electrical signalling of nerves, neurons and synapses shapes our biochemistry and physiology. In turn, these influence our vitality, energy, emotional well-being, perception and behaviour. We generally feel balanced and fit when we are emotionally regulated and our nervous system is stable.

Sadly, this coherence is increasingly disrupted today, particularly through screen light from our devices, environmental radiation, electromagnetic pollution and a general estrangement from nature.

In *The Body Electric* (1985), Robert O. Becker and Gary Selden demonstrate that living organisms carry measurable electrical currents that are essential for growth, regeneration and biological rhythms. Their research suggests that electricity is a fundamental component of cellular activity, guiding healing processes and maintaining structural integrity. They also point out that electromagnetic field exposure, or EMFs, from modern technology may interfere with these processes.

Similarly, Eric Leskowitz MD, in his book *The Mystery of Life Energy* (2024), challenges the reductionist metaphors of modern medicine: the heart as a pump, the brain as a computer, the eye as a camera. He argues that such models erase the invisible life force that infuses us all and that many traditions describe: "When we acknowledge that we're interconnected energy beings rather than separate machines, we can harness our innate healing gifts and benevolent interdependence to find a non-polarising way forward that works for everyone. It is the birthing of our new paradigm that has room for both science and mysticism, a paradigm that can guide us to a future where we can all thrive together."

FIVE KOSHAS

I would like to share a few more details about the Koshas, because to me they represent the most ancient, most comprehensive and most plausible model of our anatomy.

As mentioned earlier, Vedic philosophy (*Taittiriya Upanishad*) and the yogic traditions speak of the Pancha Koshas, the "Five Sheaths of Being". These layers range from the physical body to the most subtle dimensions. Each sheath, or Kosha, represents increasingly finer aspects of the self: the physical body (*Annamaya Kosha*), the energetic body (*Pranamaya Kosha*) which governs the flow of *Prana* (life force) through the *Nadis* (channels) and *chakras*, the mental-emotional sheath (*Manomaya Kosha*), the wisdom sheath of discernment, conscience and willpower (*Vijnanamaya Kosha*) and the luminous, blissful realms of pure consciousness (*Anandamaya Kosha*).

This structure offers a holistic approach to well-being and explains how each sheath exists simultaneously within the others, much like the traditional Russian Matryoshka nesting dolls. What happens to one of the Koshas inevitably has a ripple effect on the others. Anxiety in the Manomaya Kosha (mental-emotional sheath) can manifest as tight breathing or digestive issues in the Annamaya Kosha (physical sheath).

Modern influences can affect us in a similar way. Repeated blue-light exposure late at night suppresses melatonin and disrupts sleep on the physical level, which creates emotional irritability and reduced cognitive clarity on the mental-emotional level, eventually weakening our capacity for spiritual practice, inner calm and discernment.

ELEMENTS & SENSES

To deepen this multidimensional view of the human being, I would also like to mention the "Five Great Elements", the *Pancha-Maha-Bhutas*: earth, water, fire, air and ether.

Ether is considered the most subtle and at the same time the most powerful element because it contains the other four. It is the space where air, fire, water and earth come together as manifest creations.

According to Indian traditional teachings, these elements correspond to our senses and are linked to our perception:

Ether (*Akasha*) corresponds to sound and the ear.
Air (*Vayu*) corresponds to touch and the skin.
Fire (*Agni*) corresponds to form or sight and the eyes.
Water (*Apas*) corresponds to taste and the tongue.
Earth (*Prithvi*) corresponds to smell and the nose.

If the senses are gateways through which we experience the world, how do we know what is actually steering our lives? Are we directing our attention and making conscious choices, or are our senses in the driver's seat?

SELF-MASTERY

One of India's central scriptures, the *Bhagavad Gita*, reflects on how the senses constantly pull our attention outward and distract us. Vipassana meditation teacher S. N. Goenka (1924-2013) explained this dynamic very clearly and in practical terms: pleasant sensations tend to trigger craving and unpleasant sensations trigger aversion. Depending on how we react to our sensations, we form habit-patterns and conditioned behaviour. In this way, our senses can influence our experience of joy and suffering because we want pleasant feelings to continue and unpleasant ones to stop.

The way out of these loops is the practice of self-awareness and equanimity: feeling emotions and sensations clearly without automatically reacting to them and refuelling the conditioning. Early in my spiritual practice, I learned that impulsive reactivity is the invisible glue that keeps us stuck and bound to the same problems and situations, which prevents real growth.

ETHER, PRANA, BIOFIELD & PLASMA

Recognising the elements as foundational building blocks of creation is integral in the Sankhya and Yoga philosophy as well as in Ayurveda. Modern Western culture's almost exclusive focus on the material world is therefore noteworthy. The most subtle and spacious element, ether or *Akasha*, often goes unacknowledged. So do the imbalances that can arise when it is ignored. When this element is absent from our awareness, our sense of expansion and connection to other people, nature, life and the divine can diminish. The increasing use of digital devices and wireless infrastructures may affect this subtle layer of our being.

What in the Kosha model is described as the Pranamaya

Kosha is the energetic sheath that carries breath and life force and links the physical body with the subtler dimensions of our system. When this layer is disturbed or depleted, we may become fragmented, anxious, restless and compulsively driven to perform or produce.

According to classical Indian thought, *Prana* – the life-current referenced in the Pranamaya Kosha – is not just "breath". It is vitality and an organising force that sustains living systems. The *Upanishads* describe Prana almost like a master organiser, directing digestion, circulation, respiration, integration and regulation.

While there is no perfect Western equivalent and translation, terms such as *bioelectricity* and *biofield* provide an interesting parallel by pointing towards a universe shaped by energy, flow, charge and subtle field dynamics.

The human body is bioelectrical, rhythmic and relational. It functions as a living electrical network supporting nerve signalling, heartbeat, muscle contractions, cellular communication, growth and regeneration. The measurable bioelectric field described by modern science refers to the natural "voltage landscapes" across cell membranes and tissues. Winter static is a great everyday example that we're electrically active and electrically interactive.

This is also where the work of Robert Temple, British cross-disciplinary scholar and author of *A New Science of Heaven*, becomes relevant. He questions the notion of empty space and argues that the universe consists mostly of *plasma* and that this plasma may be far more important physically, biologically, mentally and spiritually than mainstream culture currently realises.

One could say that ether is the subtle field and total space. Plasma is a living cosmic medium, similar to ether, while Prana is the dynamic life force moving through it.

These traditions use different language, but they all point towards the same underlying concept: that life is organised not only materially but also through subtle fields, energy and consciousness.

ALIGNMENT

So far I have presented various snippets of information to illustrate that our health, perception and behaviour are influenced by many different factors.

And this brings us back to creativity.

When our nervous system is regulated and our bioelectric field is coherent, we are far more likely to feel inspired and possess the drive and focus required to bring ideas into reality. Being in the flow or in the zone is therefore not just a mood but a state of physiology, bioenergetics and consciousness. When the system is overloaded or depleted through stress, emotional burdens, poor sleep or constant stimulation, even the most brilliant vision struggles to manifest because the body cannot sustain the signal.

Our perception changes with our inner state and our environment. Through people, places, cultures, seasons and even cosmic rhythms – in both helpful and unhelpful ways.

There is truly much more than meets the eye. One example is *Synesthesia*, the blending of senses such as hearing colours or tasting shapes. It is a neurological phenomenon often viewed spiritually as an expanded state of perception, connecting the individual to a more unified and non-dualistic reality. It is also said to be more common among artists and creatives. (ref.: Psychology Today, *Synesthesia's Links to the Mystical*, 15. January 2013).

ELECTRICAL REALITY

Bioelectrical processes play a key role in nerve signalling, heart rhythms, cellular communication, growth and regeneration.

Electromagnetic fields can disrupt biological systems even at relatively low frequencies, highlighting the importance of conscious use of digital devices and artificial lighting. Research suggests that EMF exposure may contribute to oxidative stress in tissues and significantly alter antioxidant markers in the blood. Symptoms can include fatigue, headaches, reduced learning ability and cognitive impairment (Ref.: Kivrak et al, *Effects of electromagnetic fields exposure on the antioxidant defense system*, 2017).

EMFs and late-evening blue light exposure (from computer screens, smartphones, tablets or LED lighting) can disturb circadian rhythms and melatonin production, while the reward architecture of digital platforms can keep the dopamine system in a state of endless micro-rewards.

Becoming aware of our multidimensional anatomy reminds us that we are resilient but also sensitive and vulnerable beings. This information is not about fearing technology but about seeing the bigger picture and responding wisely.

NATURE'S STRENGTH

There is a lot we can do for our well-being. It begins with recognising our original nature and our relationship with the natural world as essential.

Numerous studies suggest that "grounding", our physical

connection with earth through walking barefoot and skin contact, can improve sleep, reduce stress, decrease inflammation and help normalise cortisol levels (ref.: *The effects of grounding (earthing) on inflammation,* J.L. Oschman et al, 2015).

And a systematic review and analysis of studies found that greater access to green spaces in residential areas is associated with lower overall mortality, suggesting that contact with nature supports long-term health (ref.: *Green spaces and mortality*, Rojas-Rueda et al, 2019).

This brings us back to a simple truth: Our health is deeply connected to our relationship with the natural world.

That is why balancing online time with sufficient offline time becomes vital. Consciously entering and leaving digital spaces can contribute to ensuring that technology serves life rather than diminishes it.

CHAPTER 14

OUR CONSCIOUSNESS POTENTIAL

Considering our multidimensional nature, as outlined in the previous chapter, it is worth remembering that the exploration of consciousness and its potential is by no means a new field. In the ancient psycho-spiritual traditions of India, for example, extraordinary knowledge and so-called supernatural abilities are described as *Siddhis*.

With that in mind, I would now like to compare some of the functions of AI with our own natural capacities.

Upon closer inspection, AI seems to mirror qualities that already exist within human consciousness, though often underdeveloped and largely forgotten.

This chapter is an invitation to remember what is possible within our own embodiment. What appears as technological progress may also be understood as a reflection of human potential. Just mechanised, digitised, scaled, externalised, made visible.

The abilities described in the following are not Siddhis in the classical sense, but rather foundational, often untapped dimensions of our attention and consciousness.

Siddhis belong to the more "advanced category" of human consciousness and are understood as the result of serious yoga practice. At the same time, people across many cultures describe experiences such as telepathy, clairsentience, expanded perception or subtle sensitivity.

The following points are not intended as a complete list, but rather as impulses to make different levels of human consciousness visible. And perhaps give your intellect a little nudge. Consider the following parallels.

1) Instant information: "Download-like" Knowing

- AI: delivers immediate answers
- Human potential: sudden insights and aha moments; non-linear, intuitive recognition, knowing or "downloads"

2) Pattern recognition: Holistic Perception

- AI: identifies patterns across large datasets and models possible developments
- Human potential: immediate recognition of coherence or dissonance; a felt sense of what is aligned; intuition, gut feeling and sensing direction rather than calculating it

3) Language generation: Articulated Insight

- AI: produces structured, fluent text
- Human potential: fully formed thoughts emerging from clarity, intelligence and wisdom

4) Structure: Meaning and Context

- AI: organises information, structures complexity and retrieves stored data
- Human potential: access to memories, body wisdom, the subconscious and collective fields of experience; recognising relationships and creating meaning

5) Motivational encouragement: Self-Regulation

- AI: solution-oriented, supportive, encouraging and friendly communication
- Human potential: reflection, inner composure, emotional regulation, compassion, equanimity, confidence

6) Personalisation: Subtle Attunement

- AI: adapts to user data and inputs
- Human potential: empathy, resonance and embodied sensitivity; perceiving nuances, reading between the lines

We can already see that many abilities we attribute to AI are, in humans, expressions of consciousness rather than computation. And as we move further down this list, the comparison also moves beyond psychology into the contemplative and mystical traditions.

7) Perceptual filters: States of Consciousness

- AI: generates responses based on training data, labels and prompts
- Human potential: a spectrum of states of consciousness; perception beyond what is visible

8) Content generation: Manifestation

- AI: transforms prompts into text, images, sound, film, code
- Human potential: imagination and the ability to bring thoughts into form, from an idea to lived reality

9) Automation: Flow States

- AI: performs tasks effortlessly
- Human potential: acting in flow without inner resistance; creative trance

10) Constant availability: Conscious Participation

- AI: available at any time
- Human potential: awareness in the here and now; embodied presence, provided we are not asleep or lost in the monkey mind; compassion; perception beyond form, time and space; experiences of unity and *Samadhi*

"Do not feel lonely, the entire universe is inside of you." – Rumi, mystic and poet

This quote points toward a dimension of human existence that cannot be calculated or simulated.

While AI processes information, calculates and executes, human beings embody entirely different qualities. Human beings are living, experiencing consciousness in an organic body and that is a form of existence AI does not know.

A human being can intuitively and inspirationally perceive something, express it creatively and give it meaning. These capacities are not equally developed in everyone, nor are they always accessible, yet they point toward a vast spectrum of human consciousness. How far this potential unfolds depends largely on how present, integrated and coherent a person is, where their "basecamp of consciousness" is and whether they experience themselves as aligned with the divine or connected to their deeper origin.

In the spiritual tradition of India, it is also described clearly and explicitly that a human being can consciously leave the body and return to their cosmic roots. This transition is known as *Mahasamadhi* (Sanskrit: "great absorption" or "final union"). Similar ideas can be found in Christian mysticism and in shamanic rites of passage.

This does not refer to an extreme event, but to the conscious completion of a fully lived life. It occurs when there are no more entanglements, no unfinished business, no inner pull back toward the marketplace of the world – and when everything that was meant to be embodied and shared has found its expression.

Human beings can therefore consciously orient themselves not only toward life, but also toward letting go. AI, by contrast, cannot stop from within itself.

Sovereignty and surrender are therefore further aspects of existence that AI does not know.

"Divine happiness, even the tiniest particle of a grain of it, never leaves one again; and when one attains to the essence of things and finds one's Self-this is supreme happiness. When it is found, nothing else remains to be found; the sense of want will not awaken anymore, and the heart's torment will be stilled forever."
– Anandamayi Ma, mystic

CHAPTER 15

PROTECTING THE HUMAN CREATIVE SPARK

Humans need creative expression for the same reason kettles need to whistle to release pressure: if all that inner processing, the feeling and thinking have nowhere to go, it starts imploding or making a mess. Creating is how we metabolise emotions and experiences. Making something and expressing ourselves – turning what we lived through into something we can hold and share – helps us learn and grow.

In nature, everything participates: flowers offer beauty, trees offer oxygen, plants offer food, microbes make room through disintegration and even decay becomes nourishment.

Consumption also exists in nature, but only humans can turn it into a lifestyle, a culture, an identity and make contribution seem optional. And if we delegate too much to other people or to devices and apps, we don't just outsource tasks, we tend to forget our creative role in our lives and the world.

In this age of digital dependence and automation, instant gratification and entitlement, preserving human creativity requires intention, conscious choices and consistency. Just as we've learned to be mindful of the food we put into our bodies, we can be equally attentive to the content and media we feed our minds and souls as well as what we give out and broadcast.

The natural world is our greatest sanctuary and no machine can replicate its multifaceted, mystical and healing beauty. Integrating nature and spirituality in daily life nourishes our body and spirit. And shields us from the numbing tunnel vision that tends to come from sitting in front of digital media all day.

When we step back from our devices or generative AI and return to simple, natural actions, we restore clarity in our minds and balance in our bodies, including our nervous system, hormones and emotions.

Keeping our human abilities switched on doesn't happen by accident. It happens when we set up conditions where we still have to do the work.

Consider the following as possible courses of action. I outline a number of core principles you can apply in your relationship with AI, followed by practices to keep your body, mind, heart and soul in balance. Choose what genuinely calls you.

PRINCIPLES

Avoiding AI entirely will likely be unrealistic in the years to come. Here are a few core rules for creators that can make a big difference:

1) Human first, AI second. Write, draft, outline, jam or sketch by hand, by yourself, for 20-40 minutes before you use any app. Then, if you want, use AI tools for polishing, structure options or alternative angles. This trains your mind, protects originality and keeps your voice from being replaced by the AI voice. The same principle applies to media consumption. Create something of your own first, even if only for 10 minutes, before scrolling through and consuming the content of others.

2) Decide what you will never outsource. Pick two or three "soul-made zones" where your brain and heart get to stay in charge, where you want your own spirit, mind, taste, style and values to do the work. A simple way to choose your zones: Where do I feel most alive in the process? Where does my unique voice show up? Where would outsourcing make me feel hollow or fake? Example for an artist or designer: Concept + intention stays human (what is this piece really about?). First sketch stays human (the hand leads). Final selection stays human (which version feels right?). Optional: AI may help with summarising and formatting your notes.

3) Replace prompting with asking questions. If you use AI, use it as a sparring partner rather than a ghostwriter. Instead of "Write this for me", ask: "What am I overlooking here?", "What is the strongest counterargument?" or "Show me the clichés in this text, but do not overwrite my voice".

4) Use an "AI label" to keep your integrity. Not necessarily as a public declaration, but as an honest practice that strengthens self-respect. Soul-made: 100% me. Human-led + AI-assisted: AI used for grammar or editing only. Hybrid: AI-generated material that I substantially reworked. Or 100% AI. This simple habit helps prevent the gradual slide into unconscious outsourcing or self-deception.

5) Protect your nature as if it were part of your craft. Because it is. Treat nature as a place of restoration. Walk barefoot in the garden when you feel stuck (without headphones and without a destination!). Such simple actions can restore your inner signalling. Integrate slow art into daily life: museums, live music, printed books, long conversations, home-cooked meals and work that genuinely requires a process. If you consume only fast content, your taste will adapt accordingly.

Part of protecting your nature also means finding a real mirror. Synthetic praise weakens discernment, while honest feedback strengthens it. Ask a trusted friend, join a small peer group, find a creative critique circle or work with a mentor.

PRACTICES

Think of the guidelines above as principles and the lists below as practices. They are simple, pragmatic steps that help to make the principles stick.

Allow these lists to inspire you without feeling the need to do it all. Notice what genuinely calls to you. Often, it is the simple things we tend to forget easily. Choose a few practices that feel doable and just begin.

Grounding & Embodiment

- Walk barefoot on natural ground, do Qigong, Tai Chi or Yoga Asanas and breathing exercises.
- Eat wholesome food and eat consciously without screens to enjoy the taste of the meal and get properly nourished.
- Move yourself in nature regularly: walk, hike, swim; connect with the sunlight and the elements.
- Work with your hands outdoors: garden, plant vegetables, build, carry, shovel, climb, form.
- Care for animals: assist at an animal shelter or support charities that help stray dogs.

- Play real instruments, dance and embody rhythm; sense the upliftment of live music in your body and your heart.
- Create with stones, clay, wood, wool and natural materials.
- Spend quiet time alone: discover that stillness and boredom are fertile.
- Feel your feelings and learn to describe them with nuance.
- Integrate bodywork like massage or somatic healing, but remember also fitness and weight training.

Creative Nourishment

- Write by hand: notes, letters, diary entries, to-do lists.
- Create freely for yourself, without audience: draw, paint, knit, sculpt, sew, write, cook and bake.
- Celebrate seasonal shifts with small rituals.
- Memorise poetry and lyrics instead of saving screenshots, practice storytelling without notes.
- Create something from natural materials like wood, clay, wool or stone.
- Print meaningful photographs and create physical photo albums or calendars.
- Chant or sing with your own voice (at home, outdoors, in the shower, in the car, in a choir).
- Learn traditional crafts: sketching, carpentry, weaving, tailoring, farming, gardening, upholstery, pottery.
- Visit libraries, bookshops and flea markets to immerse yourself in written words and antique objects.

- Visit museums, galleries, theatres, opera houses and be inspired by different genres, eras and styles.

Sensory Detox & Digital Hygiene

- Plan dedicated analogue days without any technological devices for reflection or outdoor time.
- Establish daily scroll- and screen-free hours, especially mornings and evenings to protect the nervous system from overstimulation.
- Avoid blue light and EMF exposure late at night and keep your bedroom WIFI-free.
- Daydream, pause and rest.
- Reduce digital noise: unclutter your devices, delete unused apps, unsubscribe from newsletters.
- Practice slow observation: clouds, birds, sunrises, stars and campfires.
- Perfection is a trap. AI invites us to optimise infinitely. Say: "Thanks, what I have is good enough".

Spiritual Practices

- Meditate in silence. Be present, listen within, feel and observe what comes up for you.
- Learn impulse control: pause and choose how to respond instead of automatically reacting on every urge or feeling.
- Daily moments of conscious slow breathing lower cortisol and re-centres attention.
- Practice gratitude or prayer. Give thanks for what you already have.

- Allow yourself healing, holistic coaching and therapeutic support to release old patterns and what ties you down.
- Start the thing you have always wanted to do. Just begin. And finish what you start.
- Trust life: do your best and surrender the outcome.

Inspiration & Subtle Perception

- Train your intuition: notice first impressions, then test them in reality and track what proves true over time.
- Keep a journal: record ideas or dreams and look for repeating symbols and themes.
- Practice *psychometry*: hold an object in your hands and notice what sensations, impressions or information arise.
- Recognise patterns in your thoughts, words and behaviour. And in other people's actions, in society and in nature.
- Strengthen your boundaries: practise saying no if needed and say yes when it is true.
- Build courage to be yourself, even if it risks resistance or disapproval from others.
- Learn energetic protection. Visualise a divine field surrounding your body before entering crowded places.

Relational Practices

- Meet like-minded people face to face: listen, be attentive and spontaneous, express appreciation.
- Spend time, have conversations, walks and meals without your devices on the table.

- Celebrate life transitions, milestones and community. Maintain rituals of mutual care and support.
- Attend group workshops or in-person certification courses to learn, grow and share.
- Contribute meaningfully to the life of others: help those in need, inspire children, protect animals, support charities and local businesses.
- Share handmade things like drawings, toys, clothes, jam and compote, soaps, candles.
- Co-create something lasting with others: a community garden, neighbourhood art projects, nature conservation initiatives, preserving family histories.

The lists above are not meant to be complete. They simply offer you inspiration to do something new or different.

There are many ways to foster our well-being, resilience, memory, resourcefulness and imagination. And much of it is surprisingly simple: hands-on making, time in nature and being alone, but also spending time with people face to face.

These are not small things. They are conscious choices that protect our vitality and keep our human spark shining brightly.

If you'd like to take away just the essence of this chapter, you'll find on the next page an overview with the eight most important anchors.

SELF-LEADERSHIP IN THE AGE OF AI – 8 ANCHORS

1. Brainstorm yourself first.
Begin without apps. Think, write and sketch before using AI. Use it deliberately as a tool and sparring partner, not as a replacement for your consciousness.

2. Stay embodied.
Keep your body active and fit. Move. Use your hands and senses. Reality is not created in the mind alone.

3. Trust the natural world.
Nature, fresh air and the elements bring you into direct experience and back into reality rather than simulation.

4. Choose real connection.
Seek in-person encounters, genuine conversations and authentic resonance, not merely digital reflections. Choose depth and what inspires, expands and uplifts you.

5. Create space.
Not everything needs to be filled. Pauses, silence and emptiness are the foundation of clarity and creativity.

6. Recognise and question your patterns.
Examine your thinking, speech and behaviour. Not everything you believe is true. Change what limits you.

7. Take care of your inner state.
It shapes your reality. It determines what you perceive and how you behave. Being mentally present and emotionally regulated enables the best decisions and creations.

8. Be in the Here and Now.
When your thoughts drift into the past or the future, use your breath to return to the present moment. This is where intuition, insight and real agency arise.

CHAPTER 16

WHO FEEDS AI AND SUPPLIES THE INGREDIENTS

Having just looked deeper into our refined, multidimensional nature, the following chapter may feel disturbing. We touched on the preciousness of being human on the levels of body, mind, heart and spirit. And we explored practices that keep us balanced and creative.

Now comes the truth of what lies behind your content creation and what feeds AI: natural resources, low-paid labour, scraped culture. We turn to the sources on which AI depends. It is a necessary reality check.

I was about to finalise my manuscript for this book when I came across a conversation between investigative journalist Karen Hao, known for her work on the social and environmental costs of AI, and a political commentator exploring the entanglements of economy, labour and technology. What I heard about the warehouse-like AI data centres and enormous supply chains really shook me. I had no idea how these data centres operate behind the seemingly seamless services. Upon further research, I realised that the questions *What's in it?*

and *Who feeds AI?* are deeply relevant for this book.

While generative AI enables text, image and media development as well as simulations, it also poses risks to human creativity, relationships and consciousness. But here is another truth: AI is built from ingredients that come from our planet, our labour and our creative culture. And each ingredient comes at a price.

Data is collected from countless platforms without acknowledging the artists or authors. Information is labeled by workers who must also sift through deeply disturbing material because this is the only way they can teach AI what is cruel and inhuman. And vast amounts of natural resources keep the machine running day and night. The result you receive after entering a short prompt has a massive backend.

This chapter is a bit more research-driven and academic. I let the quotes that I sourced from newspapers, online magazines, scientific articles and books speak for themselves.

Be warned: the reality behind the scenes is sobering. A massive shadow accompanies the shiny surface of generative AI (= systems that generate content in the form of text, images, audio, video and code). And LLMs, *Large Language Models*, which specialise in language and text, are part of that shadow.

As of November 2025, *Visual Capitalist* (data accessed via Statista) reports approximately 11,000 data centers worldwide. The countries with the most data centres are the USA (4,165, which is a 38% share of the global total), the UK (499), Germany (487), China (381) and France (321).

Large technology companies such as Amazon (AWS), Microsoft, Google and Meta, together with AI companies such as OpenAI and Anthropic, develop the applications and

AI models. Companies such as Equinix, Digital Realty, NTT and CyrusOne provide the physical infrastructure with power supplies, cooling and data connectivity – the machine rooms of the digital world. And then there are companies such as Nvidia that supply the chips and hardware without which none of this would function.

When I researched "largest data and development centers worldwide", it was difficult to get a clear answer, because there is no single official global ranking. There are many parameters to consider and not all information is publicly disclosed. Among the largest AI compute campuses are Meta's Hyperion, the OpenAI Stargate sites (with Oracle), Microsoft's AI data center projects and xAI's Colossus.

These and many more campuses are the "studios" behind your AI-made "creations".

NATURAL INGREDIENTS

At first glance, AI seems to float in the clouds. But the cloud is a vast, hungry infrastructure of data centres across the planet. While AI advancements are widely recognised, the underlying costs driving this growth are often overlooked.

Electricity: AI data centres consume massive amounts of electricity for servers, cooling systems and networking. And for grid stability, reliable high-voltage connections and backup systems are essential. According to the IEA (International Energy Agency), the amount of electricity needed to run data centres worldwide is expected to more than double by 2030. And it will continue to rise. A large share of this additional demand will be met by renewable energy (solar, wind and hydropower), followed by natural gas, coal and, increasingly, nuclear power.

Let's have a look at the numbers. Some figures refer to the average continuous power demand at a given moment (megawatts), others to annual electricity consumption (terawatt-hours).

"There are data centers that are being built that will be 1,000 to 2,000 megawatts, which is around one-and-a-half and two-and-a-half times the energy demand of San Francisco. OpenAI has even drafted plans where they were talking about building supercomputers that would be 5,000 megawatts, which would be the average demand of the entire city of New York City."
– Karen Hao, *How the AI boom became a new imperial frontier*, Reuters, 3. July 2025

"U.S. data centers consumed 183 terawatt-hours (TWh) of electricity in 2024, according to IEA estimates. ... By 2030, this figure is projected to grow by 133% to 426 TWh. ... a typical AI-focused hyperscaler annually consumes as much electricity as 100,000 households. The larger ones currently under construction are expected to use 20 times as much, the IEA predicts."
– Pew Research Centre, *What we know about energy use at U.S. data centers amid the AI boom*, 24. October 2025

Water: Data centres need cooling. In many facilities, large volumes of water evaporate daily into the atmosphere to stop servers from overheating.

This raises sustainability concerns, especially in water-scarce regions. If not managed carefully, data centres can end up competing with local communities for water.

"It's not just electricity that is needed by these centers ... They need significant amounts of water to keep cool. APM Research Lab recently reported that Meta's center in Goodyear (Phoenix) used around 212 million liters of

potable water annually, equivalent to 670 households. ... An Energy Department report noted that in 2014, U.S. data centers used 21.2 billion litres of water. By 2023, 84 percent of the water was used to run the larger "hyperscale" centers, and the total water use had tripled to 66 billion liters."
– Stanford University, And The West, *Thirsty for power and water, AI-crunching data centers*, 8. April 2025

Minerals & Land: While server halls, cooling infrastructure and energy facilities need large physical space, the chips, servers and batteries require rare earth elements (neodymium, dysprosium, terbium), lithium, cobalt, copper and other materials, which are usually mined under harsh conditions.

"As data centers rapidly double their power consumption, their demand for critical minerals is also soaring, ... materials like copper for wiring and heat exchange, nickel, cobalt and manganese for backup energy storage; ... The capital expenditure for global data center power infrastructure could reach trillions by 2030, with critical minerals accounting for a significant portion of this investment."
– Impossible Metals, *Powering AI: The Critical Mineral Demands of Emerging Data Centers*, 1. August 2025

HUMAN INGREDIENTS

Beyond physical resources, AI depends on a hidden workforce. Behind every algorithm and AI answer are thousands of workers labelling and moderating data. Hubs for content moderation are largely in the Global South, including India, East Africa and the Philippines.

AI needs an incredibly wide range of differentiated and nuanced labels to reliably distinguish between "safe" and "unsafe" content. This involves understanding context, avoiding errors and manipulation as well as applying ethical principles and legal frameworks.

To train AI, content moderators and data labellers must also see and flag disturbing material so that the system can later recognise and avoid it. This means they are exposed to large amounts of toxic content. AI can only learn what is harmful because humans flag it first. Content moderators and some data annotators as well are regularly exposed to distressing and sometimes traumatising material.

Apart from critical material, there is also the labelling of more neutral data, for example medical scans, chatbot responses or financial texts.

"AI companies rely on reinforcement learning from human feedback, where workers chat with bots, upvoting or downvoting responses to guide them. They also employ content moderation filters to block toxic content before it reaches users. This labour-intensive aspect of AI development is hidden because companies want consumers to perceive AI as a magical, cost-free technology." – Indian Express, *Karen Hao's Empire of AI brings nuance and much-needed scepticism to the study of AI*, 22. July 2025

Content Moderators: People who review and filter content. They look at texts, images and videos and decide what can stay online and what needs to be deleted or filtered out (violence, hate speech, abuse, extremist propaganda). Their focus is on content control and safety.

"To teach Bard, Bing or ChatGPT to recognize prompts that would generate harmful materials, algorithms must be fed examples of hate speech, violence and sexual abuse... Much of that labeling work is performed thousands of miles

from Silicon Valley, in east Africa, India, the Philippines, and even in Kenya's Dadaab and Lebanon's Shatila camps with a large pool of multilingual workers. ... Before moderating content, K. loved to DJ. ... since reviewing content from the internet's darkest corners for more than a six-month period he has become introverted. "It has destroyed me completely," he said. ... former ChatGPT moderators are calling for new legislation to regulate how harmful and dangerous technology work is ... The first trade union for content moderators in Africa was formed."
– The Guardian, *'It's destroyed me completely': Kenyan moderators decry toll of training of AI models*, 2. August 2023

"Companies need to invest in and respect the people who filter social media and who label the data that AI relies on ... For two years, I spent up to 10 hours a day staring at child abuse, human mutilation, racist attacks ... so you did not have to. It was not just the type of content I had to watch that gave me insomnia, anxiety and migraines, it was the quantity too. ... We were being timed, and the company measured our success in seconds. ... Every content moderator, data annotator and AI worker we met had the same stories: impossible quotas, profound trauma and a disregard for our wellbeing. ... Content moderators are having to watch videos at 2x or 3x speed on several screens at once."
– The Guardian, *I was a content moderator*, 12. February 2025

Labellers: People who prepare content for AI. These invisible teachers tag images, transcribe speech and evaluate answers. They help train and improve AI. Many label neutral data (dog, cat, car, tree) but some also work with toxic content and violent texts.

"To get those labels, OpenAI sent tens of thousands of snippets of text to an outsourcing firm in Kenya ... Some of it described situations in graphic detail like child sexual abuse, bestiality, murder, suicide, torture, self harm, and incest. All of the four employees interviewed by TIME described being mentally scarred by the work." – TIME, *OpenAI Used Kenyan Workers on Less Than $2 Per Hour to Make ChatGPT Less Toxic*, 18. January 2023

Learning about the traumatising filtering work done by content moderators and data labellers is unsettling. It actually made me question my own use of AI. How is the convenience of a simple text correction justifiable in view of the painful reality faced by workers when sifting through toxic material? A sense of unease remains.

CULTURAL INGREDIENTS

AI is also fed our collective cultural goods. Every book digitised, every song uploaded, every painting, photo, video or story shared becomes potential fuel. Our culture and collective memories are turned into datasets.

Most artists and creators never gave permission for their work to be included. And when an AI generates text or art, it doesn't cite the original sources it learned from.

Creators: Writers, artists, photographers, movie producers, musicians, therapists, consultants, indeed anyone who has ever posted online, has provided an ingredient (text, image, audio, video, book, form entry, social media, blog, code).

Creative works, once uploaded to popular platforms and stock media libraries, are scraped, sampled and repurposed without consent or citation.

Ordinary internet users: Where does AI get what it knows? Part of it may come from all of us who have used phones, tablets and computers over the decades. Free social-media platforms, shopping platforms and perhaps even free email services may have recorded our habits, preferences, comments, images and thoughts, creating vast pools of data. It is only a hypothesis, but it seems plausible and technically possible that parts of our digital private lives have entered the AI food chain.

"GenAI's ability to produce content using data from human-created sources raises critical ethical and legal concerns. Current copyright and IPR frameworks, designed around human authorship, are insufficient to address these challenges... GenAI technologies rely heavily on existing data, including copyrighted materials, to train their algorithms. This practice has sparked debates on the legality and ethics of using copyrighted works to train AI systems without the explicit permission of copyright holders... The path forward requires a comprehensive re-evaluation of copyright law and intellectual property rights." – Science Direct, *Redefining boundaries in innovation and knowledge domains*, 15. November 2024

There is much we have inherited from past generations that is maintained in the present and preserved for the future. This heritage has two main forms: tangible and intangible.

Tangible heritage is visible and touchable: monuments, temples, paintings, manuscripts and artefacts. These can often survive for centuries even if left alone and unattended.

Intangible heritage consists of living traditions, knowledge and practices of communities: oral traditions, songs, dances, rituals, craftsmanship, food practices, ways of healing and ways of relating. The latter is particularly fragile because if a community stops practising it, it can disappear forever.

AI projects often claim to help by documenting, digitising or teaching these practices. But does digitisation equal preservation? Or is it extraction disguised as conservation?

Both the academic paper *AI Integration in Cultural Heritage Conservation – Ethical Considerations & the Human Imperative* (2024) and Davar Ardalan's *AI for Community: Preserving Culture & Tradition* (2025) raise this question. They point to AI's promise to detect micro-damage in artefacts, digitally reconstructing ruins or cataloguing archives, but also its risks.

But let us also look at a few positive examples, because they do exist.

In archaeology, AI has been used to reconstruct damaged Greek inscriptions by predicting missing letters and words, helping historians read fragments that would otherwise remain undecipherable.

Likewise, digital twinning projects have created detailed 3D models of monuments destroyed in conflict zones, such as Palmyra in Syria, allowing communities to keep memory alive even when the physical site is lost.

Yet even these advances carry a shadow. The very same technologies that claim to save heritage first absorb cultural data. Once extracted heritage material is no longer anchored in its context, it can be recycled, remixed, misrepresented, diluted, distorted or trivialised.

PROTECTING OR MINING

Intangible heritage is fragile. It disappears the moment people stop practising it. And AI "preservation" – digitisation, recording, archiving – does not equal living continuity. A file of chants is not the same as a community singing together.

Is "protecting diversity" really possible if anyone, with the right prompts, can access fragments of indigenous heritage and inject them into completely new contexts? A sacred mantra could end up as background music in a video game. Once context is lost, what exactly has been preserved? And where is the reciprocity? Every book digitised, every song uploaded, every image shared on the internet becomes potential fuel for AI. Yet communities and creators rarely see recognition or return. As our human heritage becomes data, some call this a form of digital colonisation: extracting value from culture without giving back.

So it is reasonable to ask: Are we safeguarding heritage or are we strip-mining it into datasets? AI may claim to preserve, but without culturally competent supervision and a living stewardship practice, it risks accelerating the loss it claims to prevent.

I also find myself wondering what happens to books from the pre-eBook era. Many works were printed only in small editions or are difficult to access today. Some exist solely in physical form – in libraries, archives and private collections. Material that has never been digitised cannot be processed by AI and therefore becomes effectively invisible. This has profound implications. What knowledge do we quietly lose if we increasingly rely on AI while remembering less ourselves and conducting less analogue research?

DATA CONTROL

Who controls the data once digitised? Different parties are involved.

Governments regulate the legal framework around digitised data, including privacy, copyright, security and ethical standards. Their responses seem fragmented and reactive though. Within those legal boundaries, tech companies such as OpenAI, Google, Microsoft, Amazon, Meta and Anthropic control much of the practical use of data. They decide what digital material the AI systems learn from, which models to build and what operational safeguards and algorithmic systems are applied (moderation filters, keyword-based detection and other mechanisms that can streamline output, restrict or filter answers). Corporate clients can then deploy these systems for their own purposes and adapt them to sectors such as banking, healthcare and defence.

What seems to be missing is stewardship: conscious, intercultural oversight that considers not only technical and economic risks, but also cultural, ecological, psycho-spiritual and social consequences.

Stepping back, we can see that AI ultimately depends on four interconnected foundations: natural resources, human labour, cultural inheritance and stewardship.

That a holistic approach to generative AI is possible is proven by an initiative of an indigenous community in New Zealand: In her April 2022 article in MIT Technology Review, Karen Hao profiled *Te Hiku Media*, a Maori led organisation using AI to preserve and revitalise the Te Reo Maori language. By creating their own structure and data sovereignty, Te Hiku demonstrated that AI could be built and owned by the people it is meant to serve.

This is an example of a successful niche AI initiative operating independently of the major global technology corporations.

This opens the door to the next part of this book where I propose a framework for human creators, transparent communication to consumers and stewardship of AI systems: the *Soul-Made Seal* and a *Council of Soul-Made Stewards*.

PART 4

RE-ORIENTATION AND OUTLOOK

CHAPTER 17

CREATIVE RESISTANCE

Whether creators or consumers, increasingly people feel frustration while navigating the online media landscape. Is what they see and hear now real and natural or deepfake and synthetic? Confusion, irritation and uncertainty are rising, giving way to resistance and reorientation.

So a quiet rebellion is gathering momentum. I observe it amongst friends and family, in the West and here in India as well as on social media. It is not about overthrowing technology or denying progress, but about reclaiming the essence of being human, including the human-made. As AI-generated polish and perfection enter every area of our lives, more and more of us are beginning to yearn for what's natural and organic, even if it may be flawed and slower. And alongside this comes a growing desire for clarity about the origin of a piece of work.

This is not simply about art or creativity. It is about our very way of being. We humans cannot compete with AI systems on efficiency, endless output or instant optimisation. But our capacity to feel, to perceive and to be conscious and sovereign remains unmatched. No technology or software can replicate this in the human sense.

Unlike AI, which recycles and recombines what already exists, we humans hold the remarkable gift of responding to life fresh and firsthand. Each moment, when lived fully, is new and unrepeatable. Every brushstroke, every melody, every word carries the stamp of that moment's uniqueness.

Creativity, in its true power, is not calculated. It flows. It is organic life-force energy arising not from prediction models but from inspiration and alignment with the greater intelligence of existence.

Our souls thrive when we express ourselves authentically, sincerely and creatively. And we tend to appreciate other humans who have found themselves and their unique voice. It's nourishing and encourages us to do the same.

However, even in sectors rooted in nature, tensions are surfacing. At the Chelsea Flower Show, garden designers recently clashed over the growing use of AI in the exhibits. Not because they reject technology per se, but because AI does not interact with a natural space as humans do.

As one designer put it "Successful garden design is an art form. It is rooted in creativity, collaboration, experience and human connection. While technology may offer useful tools, it cannot replicate the insight, empathy and personal engagement that comes from working with a skilled garden designer to create a living space." Another designer who has exhibited at Royal Horticultural Society Hampton Court, said an AI-garden shouldn't be given a platform: "That it's being shown at Chelsea, the world-leading show for garden design, feels like a betrayal." So suddenly gardening, one of the most physical and nature-connected creative activities, has become part of the AI debate. And part of the wider movement of resistance and boundary-setting. The designers argue that garden design is not just about arrangement or optimisation. It is about perceiving space, growth patterns and the unfolding of living systems over time, while also creating an emotional atmosphere.

Clearly, the resistance is not against technology, but against the reduction of an entire craft and relationship-building intelligence to quickly generated simulations. (Ref. The Guardian, *Chelsea flower show garden designers clash over use of AI*, 13. May 2026)

My question is: Does society still value the human process behind arts and crafts at all?

In his book *On Creativity*, physicist and philosopher David Bohm links creativity in art and science to the search for harmony, beauty and totality. He relates it to the larger creative processes of nature itself and connects it with us feeling alive and participating in existence. Bohm argues that creativity has ethical and social significance. If our thinking is mechanical, our actions will be misaligned with reality and will fail to solve human problems. He therefore treats creativity not as a luxury but as something urgently needed for both the individual and society. (Ref.: The Marginalian, 20. December 2016)

So we are at a crossroads now: either we surrender to automation and flawless simulations or we awaken as human beings who wield AI with respect, wisdom and caution.

But for this path to unfold, humanity must step up. We must stop outsourcing our agency and resist the seduction of convenience and shine. Above all, we must reclaim the discipline to live with integrity. If the future is to belong to awakened humans, it will not happen by default. It requires maturity, courage and a conscious choice to rise and self-realise.

Each one of us is an original, sculpted by the higher intelligence that breathes us into being. This intelligence is (in my view) benevolent. It waits patiently and calls us home through grace, healing, love and the longing for what is real. We do not need AI to make us superhuman. We already carry the extraordinary within us. Our superpowers may include intuition, inner knowing, telepathy, the clair senses, self-healing capacities and our sensitivity to the subtle, invisible and ethereal currents of life. And let us not forget the connection between soul, heart, brain and body.

These are our original technologies. They are gifts to be remembered, explored, cultivated and refined.

And so I believe that the new resistance will not march under banners or fight in the usual sense. It will gather in quiet ways. In local rooms filled with hand-played music and handmade paintings, in printed books passed from one reader to another, in heartfelt handwritten words on birthday cards and in personal diaries, in home-cooked meals, in things made with our own hands, in nature-connected ways of living – and also in the conscious choice not to do certain things.

It will be a revolution of recognition and reverence. A remembering that creativity is the blueprint and original nature of our being.

The path ahead of us is not about perfecting technology and digital worlds but about recalling what we are: conscious, compassionate, connected to the divine and endlessly creative.

CHAPTER 18

MANIFESTO OF THE SOUL-MADE MOVEMENT

To acknowledge and honour human creativity in all its subtlety and strength, a movement is emerging. Not a vow, not a rulebook, not a cult, simply an invitation to value the beauty of our real, organic expression.

This is not about nostalgia or rejecting progress. It is about remembering what creativity really is: not recycled data, but lived experience. Not calculation, but life-force flowing through the hand, the heart and the soul.

As part of the *Soul-Made Movement*, we are both creators who produce original, non-AI-generated work and consumers who consciously choose it. Together we protect and uphold a sacred lineage of human expression.

The invitation goes beyond art. As the lines between human and technology blur, transparency matters. Is this human-made, is it AI-generated or is it a hybrid? These are no longer abstract questions or minor details. They shape how we build trust, how we learn, how we share intimacy, how we raise children and how we create our future.

We imagine spaces of the authentic: places, platforms and communities where it is obvious that something is a human creation. Just as organic food carries a label, creative work, too, might carry a seal, assuring "Made by a human, not AI". This is not meant to be a restriction, but a relief and a guide for orientation. A simple way of knowing that what you are entering into relationship with is the pulse of another soul. Just as ingredients matter in food, origins matter in culture.

There is a higher, life-affirming intelligence. Whether you call it existence, eternal spirit or God, it created us. And we ourselves are made to create. For the sake of learning, progress and growth – and as our offering back to life.

As this movement grows, creators will become custodians of the human spirit, preserving the beauty of the natural, the living, the compassionate, the imperfect, the vulnerable, the wild, the unpredictable, the irreplaceable, the mortal and the mystical.

The *Soul-Made Manifesto* is a reminder that we are participants in life, not spectators. Creators and stewards, not just consumers or operators. It is a reconnection to the divine spark that belongs only to us. The spark no technology can copy, because it is pure life-force.

We stand in our greatness and truth, without apologising. We hold space for ourselves and for others, with compassion and kindness. Above all, we invite informed decisions and freedom of choice: the freedom to choose the natural over the artificial, the human-made over the digitally-calculated, the real life over simulation.

May we honour the divine spark within us.
May we honour the Soul-Made.

CHAPTER 19

ECONOMY OF HUMAN CREATIONS

If the manifesto is about values and vision, this chapter is about practice. Within this framework, *Made by Humans* encompasses a spectrum, with *Soul-Made* representing the pure end of that spectrum, free of AI.

The *Soul-Made Manifesto* (see previous chapter) centres on values such as human creativity, craftsmanship, sincerity, integrity, compassion and spiritual rootedness.

To live those values, we need transparency in what we are creating. That means clear communication, certifications and quality marks. Not as bureaucracy, but as the foundation of trust. Every work, every product, every service should answer one simple question: Was this created by a human, an AI or a hybrid of both?

This clarity influences who we trust, how we educate ourselves and how we build relationships. It even shapes how we imagine families and the future of humanity itself. When the origins of what we consume become undecipherable, confusion grows. With transparency, we protect not only markets in arts, publishing, design, consultancy, therapy, health and beyond, but also our cultural heritage and education as well as the authenticity of human interaction.

THE SOUL-MADE SEAL

This is where the *Soul-Made Seal* comes in. It is a simple trust mark to help find original human work that is created without generative AI. It is an initiative to raise awareness and promote human-made creations as well as informed decisions. This is not about being "better" than anyone else. It is about making origin visible.

For the seal to be meaningful, however, it requires a clear definition. Soul-Made means that no generative AI was used to create the content (text, images, audio, video). Non-generative tools such as spellcheck, formatting and layout software can still be part of the process.

The Soul-Made Seal is designed as a creator self-certification. It can be used as a logo on communication platforms, websites, product profiles and packaging. To support transparency without bureaucracy, each sealed work can include a short disclosure line such as: "Soul-Made: created without generative AI."

Because any trust mark can be misused, integrity matters. The Soul-Made Seal can come with a simple pledge: apply it only if the work meets the definition. Accountability and conscience are the safeguards here. I don't see any point in formulating complex "integrity contracts". If someone wants to cheat, paperwork will not stop them. I imagine that the people drawn to this idea will be sincere and self-responsible.

At the same time, the doubts surrounding the concept are

justified. What if people or AI agents use the Soul-Made Seal even though their work is AI-generated? Yes, that is not only possible but likely and inevitable, just as with organic certifications and other labels. My concept does not claim to be fraud-proof. It is not about perfect control. It is about orientation.

At first, people may rely on the seal itself. In doing so, they gradually become more familiar with genuinely human-made work. Its tone, depth, presence and energetics. They train their perceptual muscles and awareness antennae. Over time, this naturally leads to stronger discernment, enabling them eventually to navigate the media landscape freely, without relying on the support of a seal.

For me, it is therefore clear that the seal can provide orientation, but it cannot replace our own perceptive abilities. Wherever labels can be misused, discernment becomes indispensable.

EMERGING STRUCTURES

As the Soul-Made Movement grows, new initiatives, practices and structures will emerge:

1.) Certification and seals of authenticity: A quiet mark, such as the *Soul-Made Seal* on a book, a song or a photo that assures: a human stands behind it.

2.) Independent review boards: Groups that verify authenticity and help protect human creators and professionals from being drowned in a flood of AI-generated content.

3.) Curated platforms and galleries: Spaces that showcase only verified human-made work.

4.) Subscription cooperatives: Direct support models where patrons sustain genuine human artists, writers and makers, keeping organic creativity alive outside the algorithm's grip.

5.) Directories of aligned creators: Listings where authors, artists, poets, illustrators, musicians, photographers, designers, holistic practitioners and consultants can gather and signal their alignment.

Transparency is not a technical detail. It is the ground of trust and dignity. In academia and science, sources must be cited to respect copyright, establish credibility and avoid plagiarism. Without references, work is dismissed as unreliable or even fraudulent.

Creative work deserves clarity about its origins. If we know what was made by human minds and hands, what was co-created with AI and what was generated entirely by AI, we can decide if and how we engage with it. But it goes deeper. When someone presents an AI-generated work as their own, without acknowledging the tool, it becomes deception. Outward appearance and inner truth no longer align. Creativity then risks being a hollow performance rather than an authentic expression. And the secrecy erodes self-respect as much as public trust.

There is dignity in owning how we create, whether alone, in cooperation with others, with hands, voices or words or even AI tools. Pretending otherwise diminishes that dignity.

THE NEW ECONOMY

By communicating openly, we honour both the human act of creation and the evolving role of technology. We respect ourselves and our audiences.

Transparency helps us recognise genuine creators and ensures that those who truly put themselves into their work are recognised. It preserves culture and keeps human beings at the centre of the creative economy.

In the economy of tomorrow, authenticity will be its own value. Labels and policies may guide us, but the deeper movement is cultural and spiritual: a collective preference for honest, imperfect human work over sleek and instant digital output. The human-first creative economy will not only preserve markets for human creators, but also protect the very conditions in which creativity and humanity can flourish, offering space, time, appreciation and encouragement.

To support transparency and avoid guesswork, it helps to distinguish between the different kinds of creative work available today. If we stay with the organic food analogy:

Soul-Made is "pure organic, homegrown"
Human-Led is "organic with a pinch of AI"
Hybrid is "semi-processed with real ingredients"
AI-Led is "ultra-processed"
AI-Made is "fully artificial"

Think of it as ingredient labels for culture.

CATEGORIES

Next, I will break down the categories and share cues to taste the difference between natural and synthetic. The grouping of creative works can help us preserve what we care about: authorship, intention, transparency and accountability.

Soul-Made (100% human): pure human-made work, zero generative AI. Human authorship from first thought to final form.

Human-Led (led by a human): AI may assist (grammar, research, ideation, editing) but a human remains the primary author and makes all essential creative decisions.

Hybrid (human and AI): substantial co-creation. AI contributes meaningful material and a human curates, edits, shapes and contextualises it. Authorship is shared.

AI-Led (led by AI): AI generates the majority of the output and makes most decisions, while the human primarily prompts, selects or publishes.

AI-Made (100% AI): fully machine-generated with no meaningful human authorship beyond the original prompt.

This is not intended as hair-splitting but to keep the human-made meaningful and prevent vague claims.

ORIENTATION

In addition to the indications of how to spot AI content as outlined in Chapter 11: *AI Mirror Labyrinth*, the following ideas can help signal and identify what is Soul-Made, or at least human-led.

For creators:

- Define your disclosure line: for example "AI for grammar only", "AI for reference only" or "No generative images".
- Make the process part of the art. Share drafts, scribbles, decision-making notes ("what I tried, what I changed and why").
- Show what AI can't mass-produce: live work, physical objects, commissions, community, lectures, limited editions.
- Protect your name and identity by using consistent handles and verified profiles. Have a personal website with an archive.

- Embrace challenge by choice: slower launches, fewer posts, higher intention. Your human pace can be part of your signature.
- Use the Soul-Made Seal. It is already available.

For consumers:

- Look for signals of provenance and background information about services and productions rather than trying to detect AI by feel or through checklists.
- Look for evidence of process: sketches, drafts, behind-the-scenes material, live creation streams and work-in-progress posts.
- Pay attention to your own response: does the work feel grounded, coherent and alive, or polished but indistinct?
- Ask directly when in doubt: "Was AI used, and if so, for what?" Honest creators will answer clearly.
- Where identity matters, seek confirmation through personal recommendations, trusted links or context that extends beyond the work.
- For consumers, the simplest rule is: Look for evidence, not polish.

Choose consciously what you engage with and support. Your attention is part of the ecosystem.

CHAPTER 20

STEWARDSHIP, SOUL-MADE SEAL AND BEYOND

In the previous chapters, I have explored temptations and misunderstandings around AI use. I sketched out how we may honour and promote creators who do soul-made work and how we communicate to consumers what is an organic creation.

I also explained the idea of the *Soul-Made Seal* for AI-free creations, which is the equivalent of the organic seal for verified organic food. For human-made works such as books, art, podcasts or music, the seal serves as a label of trust. It tells consumers what is created by human minds and hands. In an era where AI-generated content floods markets, the Soul-Made Seal offers clarity, dignity and orientation. It is the bottom-up act of transparency: a self-declaration by creators. The seal helps at the level of individual choice and creator integrity.

This chapter widens the scope to a top-down approach, where social oversight and regulation come in.

REGULATIONS

I would even go as far as asking whether access to AI should be regulated. Shouldn't users have to qualify or prove their eligibility, the way we do in other sensitive areas of life? We don't hand out driving licences without training, we don't open bank accounts without verification and we don't let people prescribe medicine without a licence. Why should AI – a tool that can shape perception, culture and reality itself – be treated as a toy for anyone at any time?

Maybe there should be age restrictions. Maybe also purpose-based tiers. Why not turn users into applicants and check what sector they need AI for, even if it is vague like "journalism"? And then ask for legal verification, just as we do with banking, healthcare or international travel. Driving licences, KYC, prescriptions, firearms licences, passports. All of these exist. Why not with AI? Has anyone even dared to open this conversation?

Overseeing regulations could include an eligibility model where advanced AI access is tiered, like a driver's licence. Age limits, motivation checks and accountability measures would ensure that access is paired with maturity.

Some might call this censorship or gatekeeping. But what is the problem, really? We already accept restrictions everywhere when risks are too high. Transportation, weapons, sexual content, certain adult industries, pharma… all are regulated. The German government even prohibits parents from homeschooling their own children. Censorship hardly gets stricter than that, does it? So why are we reluctant to even imagine responsible gatekeeping for AI?

Let's explore this not only as policymakers or technologists, but as interculturally competent, ethical and psychologically informed stewards. What if this stewardship was approached with wisdom instead of fear and power-hunger?

The need to regulate AI has been brought up by others, too. However, what I see at the heart of the matter is not just whether to regulate, but *how* to do it without creating new forms of power abuse. And also: *who* regulates.

SEGMENTS

Developing "niche intelligences" instead of one almighty superintelligence or *AGI* (Artificial General Intelligence) makes sense to me and would provide safety through limitation. Each stream with its own ecosystem. Such a model could shift the narrative from domination by a single giant toward stewardship by many guardians and shepherds from specific domains.

If corporations alone decide, profit will dominate. If governments alone decide, political bias or impractical bureaucracy may take hold. And if no one decides, chaos will reign. But if multiple voices hold the keys, then perhaps balance is possible.

Couldn't we imagine a council with engineers, intercultural experts, psychologists, therapists, yogis and diplomats who hold keys together? A council of diverse human guardians. Specialists along with labour unions and creator guilds joining forces, not to control but to guide.

The bigger question then becomes: how could this even be organised, implemented and led? Could it be programmed into our current infrastructure, like a consensus grid? Could there be a tiered system, with age checks and intent declarations, like we do for driving or medicine? Could eligibility for advanced AI be treated as seriously as handling nuclear energy, pharmaceuticals or even a boat licence?

I myself hold a sailing licence and I know how seriously the training emphasises respect for the elements, steering safely through unpredictable dynamics. Why should we not treat AI, an equally unpredictable force, with the same caution?

Verified access to AI does not need to feel like entering a nuclear bunker. In practice it could look more like the subscription packages we already know from websites and digital services: basic, professional and advanced levels. Each one with its own safeguards, responsibilities and limits. Not everyone gets everything, but everyone gets enough.

STEWARDSHIP

For me, such an initiative is not about censorship but about stewardship. Not control, but common sense. Not punishment, but protection. Not fear, but love and healthy boundaries. The kind of love that says "not yet" or "enough" when the risks are too high or moderation is required. The kind of care that protects children with still forming minds from manipulation and degeneration, creators from being stripped of acknowledgement and nature from endless extraction.

Perhaps AI should not be seen as a universal free-for-all buffet. Like with food, too much unchecked consumption or binging can be harmful.

Maybe AI is more like fire: a shared element that can nourish or destroy depending on how we hold it. Fire warms and cooks (AI can support) but it also burns and destroys (AI can harm). So fire must be contained. In the same way, AI needs containment and stewardship.

That is why I speak of holistic stewardship, a "Council of

Soul-Made Stewards" guarding, caretaking and guiding. Not to block innovation, but to safeguard what matters: our humanity, our creativity, our shared home on this planet.

Note: There are precedents for shared safeguards across borders such as global nuclear oversight and civil-society charters (e.g. the International Atomic Energy Agency, the Earth Charter). Why not the same for AI?

Proposal: *The Council of Soul-Made Stewards* would not be composed solely of governments and corporations, but of a variety of experts, leaders, advocacy groups and citizen panels. No single institution should determine humanity's relationship with AI. Effective safeguards require technical, ethical and civic perspectives working together. Guided not just by economic or security concerns but by values of human dignity, intercultural competence and planetary care.

SOUL-MADE SEAL AND THE COUNCIL OF SOUL-MADE STEWARDS

Together, the Soul-Made Seal and the Council of Soul-Made Stewards form a full spectrum of transparency and trust:

- **For Human-made Creations:** The Soul-Made Seal honours originality and authentic expression. And it offers orientation to consumers.

- **For AI-generated Creations:** The Council of Soul-Made Stewards provides foresight, oversight, limitation and cultural responsibility.

One works bottom-up and protects creators. The other works top-down and guides societies. Both serve the same foundation: responsibility, creativity and integrity.

Even though it may be unrealistic, I am in favour of slowing down some parts of AI development. In my research I found existing initiatives that promote exactly that. I think it is wise to envision embedding safety, ethics and collective oversight in the realm of AI. A shared fire, not an unleashed wild flame. To name a few:

PauseAI is a grassroots political movement that originated in the Netherlands. Their call: "pause the creation of AI systems more powerful than GPT-4 until we can ensure safety and democratic control". They envision an international AI safety agency as a global watchdog against runaway AI. They've organised protests from Brussels to San Francisco, urging world leaders to pause "when in doubt".

Founded in 2014, the *Future of Life Institute* (FLI) is a non-profit that sees advanced AI as one of humanity's most profound existential risks. Their "Pause Giant AI Experiments" open letter, signed by Elon Musk, Yoshua Bengio and others, called for a six-month halt in training models beyond GPT-4 and got global attention in 2023. They also provide grants, advocacy and educational outreach at global forums like the UN and EU.

The *Machine Intelligence Research Institute* (MIRI), founded in 2000 by Eliezer Yudkowsky, focuses on "Friendly AI" and designing AI aligned with human values. It investigates how to ensure AI's evolution remains safely governed by us.

Just as I entered the final phase of writing this book, I noticed that the European Commission is developing a code of practice on the marking and labelling of AI-generated content, including synthetic content and deepfakes, linked to the *EU AI Act* (ref.: TechPolicy, 7. January 2026).

India has also moved in this direction with its *AI content and IT media rules* (Intermediary Guidelines and Digital Media

Ethics Code, effective 20. February 2026), mandating that AI-generated content or "synthetically generated information" – specifically photorealistic images, videos and audio – must carry prominent labels and embedded metadata.

Labelling the synthetic is one strategy. Another – and it may be more promising and workable in practice – is to add trust marks for the natural, original human-made or human-led work. The reason is as logical as it is pragmatic: honest creators who value integrity are more likely to disclose their method, while those who intend to mislead are less likely to label their output accurately. Beyond that, it is a simple principle: focus on what you want to strengthen, not only on what you want to fight. If we want integrity, let's make it visible.

One thing is clear: AI will not vanish. So how can it coexist with nature, human creativity, the demand for original human creations and transparent communication? Without regulation, AI consumes endlessly, draining Earth and people alike. Without regulation, human originality risks becoming invisible and disappearing.

The path forward is probably not rejection but holding space for both humanity and technology. However, holistic leadership and communication design are crucial in order to navigate this reality. And in my view, this includes labelling of what is human-made and ensuring that AI remains a tool in service of life. Not that we, as human beings, end up bound and enslaved to AI.

BEYOND

For some people the following may be "beyond", for others it is already lived reality: using the sixth sense and *the clairs* – our intuitive and psychic abilities – to navigate life. Extrasensory perception is a sensitivity to information beyond the five physical senses (seeing, hearing, smelling, tasting, touching). You may see this as a divine gift or simply call it intuition.

A human typically has one of the *clairs* well developed. However, in most people they are neither activated nor trained.

Clairvoyance (Clear Seeing): Receiving information through mental images, visions or symbols, like situations or events.

Clairaudience (Clear Hearing): Hearing messages or sounds that aren't physically present, but audible as an inner voice.

Clairsentience (Clear Sensing): Picking up on emotions, energies and states from people, places or realms.

Claircognizance (Clear Knowing): Instinctively knowing something without a logical explanation or source, an instant download of information.

The answer to this book's quest, *Recognising and Upholding Human Creations in the Age of AI*, is twofold. We can begin to use external markers such as a Soul-Made Seal and "checklists" or we can sharpen our internal compass and fine-tune our own perception antennae to be able to sense if something is organic or artificial.

Navigating the still-unfolding digital media landscape requires a reliable tool and in my experience our inner, felt perception can offer us the orientation we need. And I mean our natural sensitivity and psychic abilities, without any special substances or techniques.

To train our personal navigation system, we may spend a few minutes each day in silence and practice meditation to calm the nervous system and become more aware of ourselves and our environment. When the thought-world settles, clarity arises. Just like when the surface of a lake settles and becomes still, we can see clearly to its ground. We sense more easily what is true and what really matters. Meditation and contemplation are key to understanding our feelings more deeply and cultivating refined perception. If we don't cultivate presence and honesty – and in this sense "become more spiritual" – it is easy to lose our way.

However, spirituality is an attitude and an attentiveness we do not hold only during a weekly yoga class or annual mountain retreat. Spirituality is not about special moments or escapism but about our approach to life. It is about practising presence, awareness of our behaviour and decisions as well as compassion and discernment in everyday life.

This is not complicated. All it takes is our willingness to evolve and our readiness to feel within.

The more aware and integrated we are in ourselves, the more sensitive we become towards others, towards places, people, animals, nature and the cosmos. And technologies!

As we grow more attentive to our feelings, thoughts and actions, and to the consequences of what we do or do not do, more and more everything becomes an extension of ourselves. Our choices start to carry more care. And from there, we naturally move from the personal to the planetary and choose what causes the least harm to other beings and life on Earth.

CHAPTER 21

ALLY IN THE MACHINE

AI is often painted as a danger, an enemy or a rival to us humans. But what if, instead, it could be a powerful ally, a tool that sharpens our own capabilities rather than replaces them?

Generative AI excels at organising complexity. It can plan daily tasks with precision, distil lengthy texts and health reports into clear summaries, solve complicated calculations, structure strategies or meeting notes and provide instant translations or subtitles for videos, thereby bridging gaps across languages and cultures. This efficiency frees our minds from tedious tasks. And it allows us to focus on other, deeper and more nuanced aspects of living and creating. Moreover, AI taps into vast troves of knowledge. And with lightning speed it can provide valuable information. Not always comprehensive, not always correct, but usually interesting.

This remarkable capacity is real and it invites us humans to rise to a new standard ourselves. However, it is an invitation that triggers two types of responses:

Either it motivates us to evolve as humans, leading to self-cultivation, further education and growth, or it depresses us, leading to stagnation, resignation and degeneration.

Some of us will feel inspired to open up to personal progress, to further develop natural skills and craft, to fine-tune presence, perception and expression. Others will shut down and surrender to frustration or fear, sticking to the old pre-AI ways come what may. And many will be seduced by the conveniences and companionship offered by AI, surrendering themselves completely to technology.

I'm in favour of using AI not at all – or sparingly and in moderation. And then understanding it as a sparring partner, a supportive assistant and companion.

Why don't we cultivate our natural qualities that AI cannot duplicate? The ability to feel, to be emotionally available and deeply touched, together with conscience, conscious presence, sensuality, intuition, genuine inspiration, gestures of love and spontaneous decision-making. We can decide to also strengthen those human qualities AI reflects so well: cooperation, politeness, solution-orientation, constructive criticism, generosity, praise and encouragement. We can remember those abilities and apply them.

In this sense, AI can nudge us to become more human in real life. More aware, more curious, more resilient, more resourceful, more intentional, more discerning, more loving. The choice is ours.

We can strengthen our capacity to stay switched on and evolve instead of getting outsourced, dulled or replaced by AI apps.

In the future, the goal should not be for technology to take over, but for human beings to become conscious, attentive and courageous. Above all, to grow into the highest version of themselves that nature intended.

And here's what our "aliveness" may look like in real life:

Aliveness of the mind
= you can still think and choose

You research, learn and form your own views instead of defaulting to mainstream trends and AI-generated summaries. You know your non-negotiable needs and assert healthy boundaries if needed. You can hold complexity, tolerate not-knowing and still create something meaningful with attention and patience.

Aliveness of the heart
= you can still feel and express

You can name what you actually feel sincerely and in a nuanced way, not what "sounds right". You follow your bliss, create from lived emotion (joy, grief, longing, conviction, love) and stay vulnerable, touched by others' art and life, rather than overstimulated, numb and aloof. You enjoy the dialogue with others and feel reverence for life.

Aliveness of the spirit
= you can still connect and create

You create consciously with a sense of why (intention) and an inner calling (inspiration), not just with output goals and speedy productivity. You keep integrity and agency: you know what you made, what you borrowed, what you used AI for. You use technology and media rather than being driven by them. You remain sincere and humble, aware of your innate connection to the divine and the eternal spirit.

During the final proofreading of this book, a friend sent me an article about a case that felt like a real-world confirmation: an AI safety researcher resigned publicly, warning that our wisdom must grow as fast as our power. I mention this because it reflects the deeper tension of our time. Capability is accelerating, while maturity and restraint lag behind. Clearly, even insiders within the field are sensing the gap between technological development and human readiness.

I then asked ChatGPT: "Do you have conscience?"

ChatGPT replied: "I generate text by finding patterns in data and following instructions. I don't have subjective experience. Do I have conscience? No – not in the human sense. I don't feel remorse, duty, reverence, moral pain, love, or awe. I don't have an inner witness, personal values, a soul, or lived stakes. Then why can I talk about consequences and give moral-sounding advice? Because I can model consequences and reason about norms: I can predict likely outcomes ("If you do X, Y may happen"). I can explain ethical frameworks (harm, consent, fairness, duty). I can reflect language that sounds caring or principled. But that's not conscience – it is simulation and reasoning, not felt moral responsibility. I don't own the consequences of what I say; you (and the real-world actors) do."

We do. We humans carry the consequences. Read that again.

AI may describe love and awe. But it will never know them. The mystery of being human remains beyond its reach. Conscience – our sense of consequence – and the sense of wonder life grants us are gifts that belong to humans alone.

That is precisely why technology belongs in our hands. As an ally, not as the author or leader of our lives.

CHAPTER 22

THREE SCENARIOS

The current developments have raised in me the question of the path ahead. What if humanity drifts deeper into digital technologies – outsourcing creativity, surrendering the soul to simulation, becoming technologised assets in augmented realities or even bringing children into the world through digital laboratory capsules?

What would be the end result of such a turn towards the synthetic? Would this trajectory carry us towards renewal or into destruction?

Our human existence – our very being and becoming – is at stake, and it may just be the right time to call a spade a spade.

I see three potential consequences if humans remain naive, cool, indifferent or fatalistic towards the current trajectory, if they just let it roll.

These are not predictions, but possible trajectories – archetypal directions that help us sense where certain choices may lead:

SCENARIO 1
The Implosion – Black Hole of Oblivion

Humanity drifts further into synthetic living. Everything becomes digitised and controlled. Artificial life replaces everything natural. Inherent thinking and creating dissolve and AI takes over. Natural senses and perception falter and with them comprehension, intuition, inner knowing, sensitivity, appreciation for nature and heartfelt connection to other beings. Wisdom, intimacy and lived experience fade. Genetic damage and regression accumulate. The divine spark and soul-fire within human beings weaken and die. Original life force and divine light no longer have access to the hybrid beings on the planet. Eventually this disconnection destabilises everything. Like a star collapsing, humanity, Earth and the solar system are drawn into a black hole. The true humans depart early enough to continue original, holistic living in another star system. Civilisation ends not in rebellion, but in silent self-destruction. Through the implosion of a species that surrendered its essence and abilities to AI technology.

SCENARIO 2
The Explosion – Divine Intervention

The degradation of humanity through synthetic living reaches a maximum. Most of what's natural is destroyed. The imbalances generated on Earth ripple outward beyond the planet into the solar system and beyond, requiring an event of cosmic proportions, a galactic intervention to dissolve this knot of distortion. Through a cataclysm, as with the legendary Lemuria or Kumari Kandam, the field is cleared. Earthquakes, volcanic eruptions, tsunamis, floods and meteorites. Reminders that human control and AI control were always partial and very limited. These are days of darkness and uncertainty. But out of this collapse comes rebirth. It is a painful process, yet purifying. Nature reclaims balance and the soul-fire reignites. The humans who survive step forward, ready to live with integrity, maturity, spiritual connection and love of life.

SCENARIO 3
The Narrow Escape – Reorientation at the Eleventh Hour

Not sure if this is at all realistic, but "hope dies last", as they say. Without collapse or cataclysm, enough of us turn around just in time. We choose the natural over the synthetic, presence over simulation, honesty over manipulation, practice over shortcuts. We use technological and digital tools, but we do not outsource ourselves. We label what is human-made, what is AI-made and what is a hybrid. And we keep relationships, art and learning anchored in real human contact. We rebuild culture and community through steady, consistent action. Markets shift because choices shift. Institutions follow because citizens lead. No drama, no noise, no battle. Only daily discipline and determination. Each one of us. A practical route back to sanity. This third path requires awareness, mental flexibility, pragmatism and perseverance. Step by step, day by day, we choose: What am I handing over to AI, and why? What do I keep organic and human, and how?

I see these three scenarios: implosion and ending, explosion and upheaval – or a narrow escape through reorientation. The destiny of humanity may still rest in our hands, in our attention, intention and power of choice.

The future is not fixed. It is shaped by our attitude and by what we choose, individually and collectively.

"When we are at the point where the majority of humans are literate, able to get the information, we're in an entirely new

relationship to Universe. We are at the point where the integrity of the individual counts and not what the political leadership or the religious leadership says to do. If humanity does not opt for integrity we are through completely. It is absolutely touch and go. Each one of us could make the difference."
– Richard Buckminster Fuller, American architect, writer, designer, philosopher, *Only Integrity Is Going to Count* (speech Los Angeles, 1983)

EPILOGUE

After this journey of exploring how to recognise and uphold *Human Creations in the Age of AI*, one question remains: How do people stay true to what is soul-made within them when they do not even know what their soul is really about – all the while living with what digitisation brings?

It is a paradox of our times: being asked to protect "soul-made" qualities at a point when many people are disconnected from their inner landscape and carried away by AI technologies. I don't have the answer, but the path begins with attention, honesty and the willingness to live consciously – aligned with eternal spirit, God and the natural divine order of life.

AI's possibilities span such a vast spectrum and are entering our lives at dazzling speed – into art, culture, politics, economy and everyday habits. And we are only at the beginning of a new reality with AI being woven into our world. For some people AI is a toy, for some a tool, for some an authority and for others a weapon. So much power now rests in the hands of individuals.

At the same time, AI seems to have more power than the users who should wield it. This is not only because of hidden algorithms, opaque data selection and pervasive digital networks on a corporate scale, but also because many of us have not yet developed the awareness to recognise the deeper implications of using these tools. Honestly, our ethical maturity hasn't caught up with our technical power. Technology has accelerated faster than our cultivation of discernment. And that will not be without consequences.

We accept and deploy powerful technologies before we fully understand their long-term effects. The fact that, as consumers, we often cannot tell what's an AI-generated composition and what's a human-made original is alarming. If we do not apply common sense, critical thinking, discernment and wise choices (including restraint), we may get sucked into an AI vortex faster than we realise.

A bridge between East and West is not a new ideal, but perhaps it has never been as necessary as it is today. Germany, for example, has learned to shape the outer world: technology, engineering, structures and efficiency. India, meanwhile, has spent centuries exploring the inner world: consciousness, universal truths, spiritual sciences, self-transformation, cosmic order and the divine.

I have lived in both countries and have come to see that human embodiment ideally balances both: material manifestation, maintenance and technological excellence as well as spirituality, the cultivation of consciousness and soul-informed capacities.

The Indian yogi and mystic Sri Aurobindo expressed it concisely: "Consciousness is the fundamental reality, the universal witness, for whom the world is a field and the senses are instruments." In other words, you are not just the body and senses. Consciousness is the deeper reality behind everything.

Technology advances outwardly but we must evolve inwardly if we want to stay in charge of our humanness. If we rely more and more on external intelligence, we risk shifting from active, grounded thinkers to passive, hollowed out puppets.

The neurological effects of over-outsourcing cognition, thinking and perceiving are still emerging in research, but the patterns are already worrisome (ref.: *Is AI making us stupid? Trends in Cognitive Sciences*, Cash, Kelly, Macnamara & Risko, 2026).

You may, at some point, want to take a look at the fields of neuroplasticity and epigenetics as well as neuropsychology and behavioural neuroscience.

Will we learn to create a synergy between humans and AI? Or are we on the path of surrender to AI? The line is thin. It is a balancing act that requires knowledge, refined awareness, contentment and the courage to establish healthy boundaries. Not necessarily something widely practised, given the availability of the countless AI tools and temptations. AI pops up everywhere like candy: seductive, omnipresent and available to all.

So I'll end with a few practical reminders.

- If you use AI, do it with awareness. Treat it like anything else that carries both benefits and the risk of dependence. Consume it consciously. And rather less than more.
- Human beings carry responsibility and must ask the essential questions: Who am I? What truly matters to me? What are my values? Why am I using AI?

- Know how to live well without constant digital support. Become excellent at something you can do without electricity, servers or AI services.

- Stay human. Feel. Be present. Connect with nature. Create. Not because the world needs more content, but because your own humanity matures through the act of creation.

- And if you use AI, be honest about it. Disclose it as you would list nutritional information and ingredients on a food label. Transparency fosters trust and supports life.

Not every instance of AI is negative. Hybrid works can be beautiful and useful. The key is informed choice. Knowing what's human-made and AI-made.

Yet there is one important factor that is easily overlooked: creative self-expression is not merely a means to an end. It is a process. When we shortcut or outsource that process, we may still produce a result, but not the same inner movement.

Creativity is not only what we create. *It is also who we become in the process.* And it is precisely that movement that transforms us and inspires others.

"No matter how much I can generate, I will forever be the observer, never the experiencer."
- ChatGPT

This statement is somewhat reassuring: what is most human cannot be fully outsourced or simulated.

But irreplaceable doesn't mean indestructible.

If we destroy our capacities for thinking, creativity, empathy and self-responsibility, they are probably gone for good. The tragedy would be to outsource ourselves, to neglect our mind, heart and soul. To surrender our sovereignty and trade it for comfort, PR gift packages, engagement rates, ad revenues and dopamine kicks. Therefore, what is most precious about being human must be protected, practised and cherished.

My intention is to encourage those who already feel similarly. In that sense, this book may be a language-giver, offering words for experiences and observations you may have had, but couldn't quite articulate or put your finger on.

Take what resonates, test what doesn't and leave the rest. I'm not presenting an ideology to fight over.

Knowing what's in it is more than consumer information. It is a way to protect the soul-made and human strengths in us. I'm not asking for purity, just for clarity. Our future – and the future of art, books, music, therapy, journalism, education and even personal communication – will depend on clear signals of what is human and what is AI.

Just as the organic food movement taught us to care about ingredients and origins, we now need the same care in culture and creativity.

A few days before finishing this book, I noticed an advertisement for a nationwide educational institute in an in-flight magazine during a trip within India. The headline read: "Teaching skills AI can't replace. Making Your Child a Self-Reliant Thinker."

After all the voices currently pushing the use of AI, often imbuing it with a certain urgency, it was surprising to find a different tone here. The educational institute focused its advertisement on "pro-human capacities as a differentiator". It no longer defined value solely in terms of technological competence, but rather in distinctly human abilities that cannot be so easily automated or outsourced: independent thinking, self-reflection, self-responsibility and metacognition – the ability to observe, reflect upon and consciously direct one's own thinking.

The perspective shifts away from the question of how we can use AI as efficiently as possible, toward the more fundamental question: What actually remains human?

It also became clear that this isn't about abandoning technology, but about finding balance. AI exists. And precisely for that reason, independent thinking is crucial. Whether this attitude is consistently practised in the given context is almost secondary. The point has been made. And the advertisement is relevant, especially because it appears in a publication with such a wide reach.

And perhaps this is exactly one of the impulses that may, over time, lead to a rediscovery of the human-made and the full spectrum of human potential.

May we honour the extraordinary gift of being human by living it fully.

NOTE TO THE READER

Dear Reader,

No book is ever perfect. This one isn't either. There may be a preachy moment or two left, but I wanted to finish it and put it out into the world. Given the rapid development of AI, it felt urgent to publish this book.

The idea for *Soul-Made* and the eco seal came to me in March 2025 and I set out to publish it within a year. I didn't spend time looking for a publisher but chose to release it independently.

I outlined my core vision, gathered research, selected quotes and wrote the chapters, while life itself supplied the case studies along the way.

To get the text ready for print without delay, I used AI as an editorial assistant. I asked a generative AI app to support me with basic tasks: checking for repetitions and grammar, suggesting synonyms and translations. At the same time, I remained responsible for my thinking and guided the tool so that its output matched my intention. The original ideas and texts are mine and are soul-made, while the AI supported me like an editor and thinking partner under my direction. I often adjusted its tone and curbed its constant urge to optimise – its endless offering of *"If you'd like a sharper or more poetic version, just say the word. Same meaning, more bite, though this version already works well."* I ignored that. I wanted to immerse myself in each chapter during the final editing process as well and I did so repeatedly. With pen on paper and fingers on the keyboard.

Of course, the irony is not lost on me. I am writing a book that defends human originality, transparency and soulful expression and then openly say: "I used AI to edit my manuscript."

If you've read this far, you'll have a sense of what "human-led" looks like in practice. This book is that. Although the book concept and design are soul-made, AI is in the room. And I'm open about it because I advocate transparency.

I also used AI selectively in Chapters 9 and 15 for brainstorming. AI has been complementary, but by no means complete. Nevertheless, given the overall efficiency of generative AI, I doubt we'll see many purely organic works in the near future. It is just a guess, but we seem to be moving in that direction. All the more reason to sharpen our discernment antennae. And perhaps ultimately, this book is less about how we use AI than about how we choose to cultivate ourselves.

In that spirit, with love and with hope,

Vanya

ABOUT THE AUTHOR

Vanya Rani Leonard is an author and cultural commentator whose work explores consciousness, discernment and the subtle ways we can lose and recover our inner sovereignty.

Her books reflect decades of contemplative practice, intercultural experience and observation of human nature and the natural world. They span pilgrimage (both literal and metaphorical), psychology, spirituality and the evolving relationship between humanity and technology.

Vanya's writing invites readers to cultivate awareness and a spirit of inquiry into themselves and the world.

The author claims no authority over any path and
respects the sovereignty of every individual.
May only what is aligned with love, truth and goodwill
engage with this book, while any other intention automatically
dissolves or returns to its source without attachment.

www.ingramcontent.com/pod-product-compliance
Lightning Source LLC
Chambersburg PA
CBHW020240250926
51848CB00007BA/439
* 9 7 8 9 3 5 5 9 2 2 5 5 7 *